Table of Contents

Tapping into Chicks

By Aaliyah Dahlia

♥ ☮ ♪

Okay, Boys! Get in, sit down, shut up,

and hang on. We're going for a ride.

~Aaliya

It's Not Fair

It's not fair. Men are tricked. Men are duped into thinking that the way to a woman's heart is through six-pack abs, roses, wine, and jewelry. They are conned into believing that they have to be jaw-dropping sexy, well off, and substantially hung in order to win the woman of his dreams. None of this is remotely true.

If a man deems himself as inferior in the physical or financial department, he will sometimes try the *being her friend route*— hoping that if he offers a sympathetic ear and a big-strong shoulder to cry on, he will win her heart forever. I wish it were that easy.

A man who subconsciously doesn't feel good about himself might try all kinds of tricks; he shows up for a first date wearing too much cologne, foots the bill for extravagant dinners, he takes chivalry to the ninth degree, opening doors and kissing her hand instead of giving her a goodnight kiss... and for what? To have her front door slammed in his face at the end of the night as he walks back to his car with a boner. This same man will become highly attached to (said) female because men are *biologically wired* by Mother Nature to chase (a.k.a. "hunt") whatever (or whomever) eludes them. So he turns up the volume on his swoon-factor—calling and texting her wwaaayyyy too often (a surefire turnoff, boys – so knock it off!). He'll try winning her over with sappy poetry, pretty lies and flattery, bigger and better gifts (flowers, teddy bears, chocolates—whatever he thinks will woo her)... he'll start working out, running, and drinking protein shakes and gallons of water, believing that six-pack abs, along with his gift-shop labors of love will be enough to win her over.

And what does he get in return? Not a damn thing. Does she ever end up falling for him? Not a chance. However, this same woman will pine away after another guy who seems to think more of his fantasy football league—or beer can collection than he does of her. What in the... hell is going on?

When it comes to recognizing their own value, a lot of guys sell themselves short. Most identify themselves with their failures of the past—instead of their true potential in the present. If you are a man who struggles with dating, relationships, or even just *getting' lucky*, then you've got the right book in front of you. The information in this book is simple but powerful. It will help you shape-shift into the **hot** version of yourself. You will quickly be able to identify your relationship pitfalls, and, most importantly, you will learn how to quickly correct them.

True, some men will need to work at it more than others—simply because some men will have a harder time breaking their really bad girl-wooing habits and negative mindsets and beliefs. Some men are up against years of female rejection, disappointments, and harmful self-talk. However, the ideas here aren't difficult and you can begin using them right away.

Beautiful Oil Painting

If you saw a beautiful oil painting in an art gallery, you might stop to admire it. You would possibly, if you were permitted, walk up close to the painting and run your fingers lightly across the textured paint. You might even daydream about taking the painting home with you and hanging it up on your wall so you could look at it every. *Sigh...* That is such a beautiful painting...

Now, imagine that the artist of the painting walks around the corner and notices you admiring his painting. Imagine that he gets really excited and says, "Hey! Do you like what you see there, Buddy? Ain't it beautiful!?" His voice booms.

"Uh… yeah, it's great," you say, a little taken aback with the artist's enthusiastic demeanor.

The artist is so excited that you have shown interest in his painting that he walks over and takes it down off the wall. He brings it close to you and says, "Have a look! I don't mind!" He shoves the painting right up to your face. "Yeah, man! Look at my beautiful painting! You are so lucky that I am letting you see my painting this close up! Isn't it rad? What do you like the most about it? Do you like the colors I used? What about the brushstrokes? Look at it closer! Look at that genius texture I used! I'm so happy that you like my painting! You just made my whole day! Do you want to buy it? Aww, heck! You can just HAVE it! For real! I want to give it to you! Take it! Take it! TAKE IIIIT!!"

Well? What would your reaction be? More importantly, what just happened to your interest in that oil painting?

Note that the inherent value and beauty of the oil painting is **exactly the same** as it was before the artist showed up and shoved it down your throat. However, it's *perceived* value just took an immediate and dramatic nose dive. You wouldn't take that painting home and nail it to the wall now for anything!

I want you to start thinking about sexy, brilliant and supposedly unattainable girls the way you think about this oil-painting scenario. Hint: YOU are the artist. Your physical presence is your oil painting. She is the admirer. The *being harassed by the excited, overeager artist* is exactly how girls feel when sexually-starved men have no measure of self-control and close the distance between them too quickly.

This, in a nutshell, is the basic premise of this book: learning how to maintain intrigue and intense attraction between you and the women you really, really want.

This Book Was Written Specifically for Men

Tapping into Chicks will help you figure out how to get your dream girl to fall for you by making a few simple (but crucial) changes in your attitude, presentation, beliefs, and mindsets. But first, Johnny.

Baby Brother Johnny

My sisters and I had a baby brother, four years younger than me, and only one year younger than Ashley, my youngest sister. With all those females in the house, poor Johnny never saw the inside of the bathroom. In fact, one day we were all out by the swimming pool and I noticed a bar of soap and a bottle of shampoo on the diving board. "What is this stuff doing out here?" I asked.

Johnny piped up. "How do you think I get clean before school every morning, Sis?" Poor Johnny! But what Johnny lacked in bathroom space, he gained in valuable knowledge. More pointedly, he had what most males only WISHED they had—a "fly on the wall" view of exactly what makes females romantically tick. He learned what attracts girls to certain boys... and what repulses them from others. Johnny had seven sisters. And we all dated—a lot. He heard us talk about boys—a lot. He saw us gaga in love—a lot. He saw us suddenly lose interest in the clueless guy after he showed up with breath that could sedate a gorilla (*Johnny's Note to Self: Brush teeth. Floss. Use mouthwash. Always.*) or making a stupid, blubbering, idiotic remark when there was a lull in conversation *(Note to Self: If I don't know what to say, shut up and chill)* or the dude who showed up in green polyester moose-knuckle-pucker pants (moose knuckle=male version of camel toe) and a bow-tie *(Note to Self: Polyester moose-knuckle pucker: bad. Jeans and tee-shirt, good)* or our super-cool boyfriend suddenly becoming a jealous, pain-in-the-ass, cling-on-for-life-control freak *(Note to Self: Even if I really like a girl, hang back. Act cool. Give her space. Chillllll).*

Johnny heard his sisters talk about our bona-fide nightmare dates—like Mandy's guy who "showed up in a shirt that smelled like moldy B.O." (B.O.= *body odor*) *(Note to Self: Don't pull a shirt out of the wash hamper, fluff it in the dryer, and wear it, because your nick name will be "Stinky Dumb Fuck" for the rest of your life).* Mr. Dumb Fuck tried to cover up the stink in his shirt with cologne. Mandy gagged through the whole date. She ended up cutting it short, came home, and ranted about her burning nostrils for a half hour. *(Note to Self: Easy on the cologne, dude!)* This is a good time to point out that women have a much better sense of smell than men—so even if a guy can't smell his own body odor, she can. Even if he can't tell how bad his shirt smells, she can. Even if he can't smell his stinky feet, she can. (Don't believe me? Google it!)

And that cologne you just doused yourself with? Bad news... she can smell right through it—and you've now just given her two assaults on her olfactory senses. Guess what? You're not going to be tapping into that chick anytime soon.

Johnny heard us talk about "the guy who just said the stupidest thing to me about my boobs!" *(Note to Self: Tell her she's beautiful – in a non-sleazy, non-creepy way. If you like her boobs, keep it to yourself)* or who "called me five times already today!" *(Note to Self: Call (or text) her ONCE. If she likes you, she'll call back)* or the guy who *"I really liked at first, but now he's always pawing at me and invading my space and says he never wants to lose me! Holy Hell! I've been trying to ditch him all week but he won't take the hint!" (Note to Self: Even if I'm desperate, hang waaayyy back. Chill out. Hands off. Don't help myself to her titties.)*

Johnny saw us plot our avoidance of the smothering suitor who wouldn't leave well enough alone, who would show up at school or our door anyway with roses and chocolates, after being disrespected and rejected by the same sister he was trying to swoon. *(Note to Self: Don't waste your money or time chasing the elusive bitch.)*

Johnny took it all in. He saw us shake our heads and mouth the words, "No! No! Tell him I'm not home!" when one of the smothering, smelly, or handsy boys would show up at the door. Then, when a different boy would call, we would speak calmly on the phone, only to hang up and jump up and down and run into the other room exclaiming to whomever would listen, "He called! He called! Oh my gosh! He called!" *(Note to Self: If she takes your call (or texts you back) she probably likes you)* then watched us primp for hours, getting ready for a date—with a boy who was a little more elusive and distant than we would have liked. *(Note to Self: Don't go crazy trying to get her attention. A little distance (but not too much) will draw her in.)*

Johnny watched us show up for school sporting events and perch ourselves on the bleachers in hopes that our heartthrob would glance our way—away from his enthusiasm of sports—which drove us even more in love—because he was more interested in his own life than he was in dating. *(Note to Self: Stay interested in my own life. She wants a guy who isn't dumping his dreams for her.)*

...and Then JONATHAN Started Dating

I could sometimes see Johnny's wheels turning as he pondered his growing interest in girls, and would think about how he would get that pretty little brunette in his class to fall for him. And I'll be *dog-gonad* if he didn't get her to fall for him—every time!

Johnny knew the dating "game" from the female perspective very, very well. In fact, he should be the one writing this book! Sadly, he can't, because he died in 2006 from a medication error. God bless you, brother… But I feel him with me now, chuckling that big belly-laugh and encouraging me with that huge heart of his—to get this knowledge into the hands of confused and lonely men everywhere. *Consider it done, Bro…*

The Girls Didn't Stand a Chance

From the time he stepped onto the dating scene—at about 16—John had girls banging down our front door for him. They asked him out constantly. They called him incessantly. And he always had a beautiful, amazing girlfriend on his arm. Because of all this, he was downright envied by his friends. It wasn't necessarily that John was better looking, smarter, richer, or sexier than any of his friends. It was simply because John had an intrinsic knowledge of what behaviors, attitudes, and *tricks of the dating trade* attracts and hold girls' attention, and what behaviors, attitudes, and presentations repel same. He was in Estrogen Boot Camp his whole tween and teen life, after all. He paid his dues. It was time for him to enjoy the spoils. And lucky you—you have an opportunity to learn from his female prowess!

So it is with utmost respect and gratitude that I dedicate this book to my most awesome late brother, the ultimate boyfriend to some very lucky women. And as I was one of the girls in that circle of seven sisters which inadvertently taught him so well, I feel more than qualified to write this book.

Now, many years later, we sisters have all moved on to our respective life-paths. Yet, I notice a striking similarity to the attraction patterns, energy, and behaviors of men that make our *damn! He's so hot!* list, and those behaviors, energies, and deal-breakers that land him on our *ugh… what a pathetic goon…* list. In other words, the dating wisdom in this book is timeless. So learn it. Trust it. Make it part of your approach to romance. Because there is never a time in a man's life when romance, sex, and love aren't important. Ever. Never ever.

What this Book Will Do For You

SO boys, here it is: an insider's view of the female dating world. This knowledge will empower you to a whole new level, and you will be able to immediately implement the ideas herein. This book will drastically and dramatically increase your "score" factor (us women want to be "scored" by the way…). This book will even teach you how to score really well, and to be that one unforgettable lover who rocked her world and left her cooing like a baby dove. Oh yeah... we want that. Nay, we crave it. More than chocolate. More than roses. More than diamonds. And any man—hot or not, hung or not, rich or not—can deliver that to her. Yeah, you. You can deliver this to her. But it will require a shifting and shedding of 90% of the bullshit you have learned about females and the way you currently relate to them. It will require you to step into a whole new mindset of what does and doesn't blow her skirt up. Most importantly, it will require for you to shift into a radical and unwavering respect and deep appreciation of yourself. This isn't some hippy-dippy bullshit, but a real-life attraction energy that will help you fix your three ring shit show romantic life.

Here's an example: say you REALLY like a girl, and you two start texting. You get a little hot, thinking about getting with her. Instead of hanging back and allowing the natural ebb-and-flow of romance to take its course, you think like a dude, and send what you deem as a super *hawt* pic of your naked (or almost naked) self.

Dude.

No.

If you think snapping a skin-pic of yourself and sending it off to her with some rank, sexual comment is going to get her hot, you're... not. Why not? Because, Buddy! You're looking at her like she's a dude! Men are visually focused. Women are... nurture focused. It takes time to gain her trust and get her to drop her guard. Obviously, there are a few exceptions, but the girl who gets hot and starts snapping pics of herself back to you has s serious lack of self-respect. And, rest assured, she is sending these same pics to at least ten other guys. A girl like this subconsciously doesn't feel loveable or deserving of a great guy like you - and she is desperately seeking approval and attention. Now, if you want a **real** girlfriend—and not a hot emotional, manipulative mess on your hands, move along from these picture-sleazy chicks. Take some time, and find a girl who is actually worth your while.

Here's another example: a dozen roses, a Pierre Cardin shirt, and Dolce and Cabana cologne probably won't win her heart, but scoop her up after a hot and sweaty football victory game and kiss her passionately—and she'll never forget you. (Just make sure you shower before taking her to bed. Because she'll probably drag you there and start ripping your clothes off as soon as humanly possible.)

You might be wondering, *well, if hygiene is so important, why doesn't she mind the hot and sweaty football victory kiss?* That's a great question. The answer is simple: in that moment, you are living your own dreams and passions—where the "play hard, get dirty" principle is very much involved. Drawing her in to be a part of that awesome energy can hugely work in your favor. But if you expect her to be equally as thrilled with your sweaty ball sack two hours later when it comes time to *yo-dee-doh-doh,* she will probably get grossed out—and either avoid you (with no explanation) or she will silently tolerate your stinky ball sac... and the sex won't be that great. This is especially important with new relationships, before a woman is used to your natural body scent and chemistry. More on this later...

What the...What?

Women are confusing—I know. We say we want roses. But we really don't; not from a brand new dating prospect, anyway. It's too soon to be that indulgent. We say we want to be wined and dined. We do. But not by a guy with no confidence. We say we want jewelry. True. But not from a guy who doesn't know how to wipe his ass.

It's about principles and priorities here. The roses, wine, and jewelry indulgences come only after a woman is hooked on you. Gifts are not ever to be used as the *hook*. Because the only girl *hooking* will be a girl with her priorities all screwed up—which as we've already touched on above, always turns out badly for the guy.

What This Book is *NOT*

Don't worry, Boys—this isn't your typical *you dirty rat-bastard—let me set the record straight with you disrespecting women like you do* kind of book. Nor is it a *man's guide to discovering his emotions because you've currently got it all wrong* kind of book. Neither of these kinds of books will help you date high-quality girls. Though in my preliminary research before writing this book, I found plenty of both the *dirty rat bastard* and the *dude's guide to finding his emotions* books on the market. I'm sure 90% of them are bought by guys who have reached their wits end, and are desperate to try ANYTHING! They are very likely also purchased by disenchanted girlfriends or housewives who are hoping to give their boyfriend or husband a clue in the love department.

Sigh… Oh boy. Read on…

The men's relationship self-help section also had books like, *How Living the Life of a Psychopath-Prick Can Work for You.* And *How to Give Her a Screaming Orgasm Using a Spork, Peanut Butter, and a Turkey Baster.* Uggghhh… Seriously twisted, missing-the-mark books that held no real actual value for men seeking to boost their dating life. But… there they were, flooding the shelves. Very sad.

Needless to say, my bookstore romp honed my sense of urgency in getting this book written and published. And… here it is—in your hot and meaty hands. *Boom!*

Hey Hunk! Yeah, You...

So... Tapping into Chicks is a book that's kind of in its own genre. It is basically a "Hey Hunk! Yeah, you. Want to get a beautiful girlfriend? Want to attract and keep your dream girl? You can! Let me show you what you need to do," kind of book. And with that being said, I am not entirely sure how this book will unfold. I have a whirlpool of knowledge to get into your view. And need to decipher it—code by code, word by word, line by line, to give you a comprehensive look at the world of romance—from a female's perspective, which, in truth, is the only one that matters. Before it goes to publish, I am dedicated to doing just that. And if you would, look up once in a while and thank John... truly, without him this book wouldn't exist.

Do Nice Guys REALLY Finish Last?

Well, yes, they do. In a world of sharks (and sharkettes) "nice" is completely overrated and counterproductive. Rather than being *nice*, strive to be genuine.

Check this: if a man shows up for a first date with roses, it's a lovely gesture. She will be delighted, of course, will eagerly grab the bouquet, and take in a good sniff. She will say, "Thank you!" She may even give him a hug or a kiss on the cheek.

Good move with the flowers, dude! Not so fast there, Fabio. What is not seen below the surface is that this girl has just made a subconscious observation; this man doesn't think that he's good enough just showing up by himself to take her out. He needed to bring flowers to sweeten the deal. *Translation: He doesn't think he's worth it.*

This nice guy will then take her to a fancy restaurant, order fine wine, cater to her every whim, and treat her like an Egyptian Princess. Again, she is delighted with the attention. But her attraction to him gravely wanes. This is because he is giving such extreme efforts to a practical stranger. There are a few exceptions to this rule, but chances are, if you are not having any luck in love, you do not fit into the *exception* category. Read on.

What is happening here? He is following the wining and dining rules to a tee! She should be falling all over herself trying to take him to bed! Right? Um… right! But if and only IF she is already hooked on him. If and only if they have been dating a while, and the "L" word has been spoken between them (and not just in his own mind or in a rushed and desperate conversation—prompted by you). In other words, if she has lain on your chest and listened to your heartbeat, or counted your breaths while she stares at you sleeping, then yes. Bring on the roses. The champagne. The prime rib. The jewelry. Your gifts will delight her, and she is probably not going anywhere. But also... don't stress if you financially can't afford these kinds of gifts. Because, if a woman is in love with you, that won't matter.

When to Move On

But the crass little hussy in your math class? Or the snooty little secretary at the office? Or the bombshell blonde you met at the club the other night who can't return your texts in a decent time frame? Hold off on the blooms and the mignon for now. ESPECIALLY if you can't really afford it and are only trying to impress her. Because you will set precedence that you can't keep up... and you will eventually paint yourself into a financial corner. Plus, if truly she is ONLY with you because of the money you are spending, she will disappear once you can't afford the gifts anymore... or she finds a guy with more money than you. You don't want a girl like that. I don't care how hot she is. Move on. And, if it's not glaringly obvious, spending money you don't have will always backfire. Don't EVER pretend to be something or someone you're not, Buddy.

Confidence – Not Concet—is Key

A man who does not feel good about himself will try to over-compensate by beefing up his dating efforts. He will clean his car spotless (or borrow his brother's or a friend's nicer car). He will don his best shirt and shine his Italian leather shoes. He will splash on a bit too much of the most expensive cologne on the market. He breathlessly shows up at her place; she saunters out in her skimpy minnie skirt and racy five inch platforms. He thinks, *Holy shit. There is no way in hell this girl will ever go for me.* In a nutshell, he cares

WAY too much about what her opinion is of him. So he sets his mind to winning her over with his money, behavior, and a lot of effort. The over-compensation game continues, until one of two things happen; he goes broke, or she stops answering his texts and phone calls. Either way, he is devastated.

Braggarts- Be GONE!

Oh—the bragging? Please... never do it. It's annoying. Only a man with low self-esteem and a lot to hide brags about himself. And women instinctively know this. You don't need to brag. You don't need to exaggerate your accomplishments. You just need to show up as the real you. Because the real you is more than good enough—and, trust me—there's a huge **lack** of authentic men in the world… and women everywhere are craving confident authenticity.

In fact, here's a phenomenal secret to dating success: instead of bragging or worrying about how you are going to impress her, simply turn the conversation to her. Ask her questions about her life, her family, and her job. Just don't do it in an interrogating or creepy way. Most definitely, keep the conversation OFF these topics:

- Religion
- Politics
- Money
- Sex

- Her favorite sex positions

- Ex-boyfriends / girlfriends

- The STDs that you picked up from your slutty ex

Pretty much everything else is fair game. If she has a pet, she will want to talk about it. If she has kids, she will most definitely want to talk about them. If she is in college, ask her about it. Has she ever been sky-diving? Be interested. Most chicks love to talk about themselves. Find out what lights her up—and talk about it. Just don't go overboard. Or turn it into an interrogating conversation.

Hygiene is Crucial

I want to take a good look at the concept of hygiene here, because it is, by FAR one of the **biggest contributors** to men's dating problems. Most men assume that there is nothing wrong with their hygiene habits. They shower every day. They shave. They use deodorant. They put on clean clothes. What could be the problem? But even men who think they have good hygiene need to pay attention. Boys, I repeat: women (especially young women of child-bearing age) have a *far superior* sense of smell than men do. In fact, scientific studies show that it is far more difficult for men to cover up body odor with a secondary scent (like cologne) because women can smell right through it… and men can't. This is HUGELY important for you boys who opt to just spray on cologne instead of showering before your dates! This is why, in the case of Mandy's "moldy B.O." guy, she could smell his stinky shirt—right through his terrible cologne... and he couldn't. Poor Clueless Stinky Dumb-Fuck… he had no idea why he couldn't get lucky. Ever.

So if you think that using soap and a **washcloth** during your shower is optional, think again. Because, based on the concept of pheromes and attraction, if a woman is not used to your skin's natural scent, even the slightest whiff of it has the potential to shut her interest down forever.

Now, obviously, this doesn't mean your natural scent is repulsive, it just means that she isn't used to it—and until she gets used to it and emotionally and hormonally bonds with you, your subtle smells can literally trigger a biological *repulsion* response. This is a survival mechanism. Quasi-sloppy hygiene habits can cause untold attraction problems for you—especially if the girl you are dating is reeling from even a semi-recent romantic breakup. Why? Because you don't smell anything like her last boyfriend, and this subconsciously signals a "change" or "threat" pattern in her brain. (Translation: *Danger! Danger! I gotta get outta here!*) This problem can be solved by you taking the time to give yourself good, soapy scrubbing right before your date—of every crack and crevice—including behind your ears, in your ears, all the way from your butt crack and beyond, to your arm pits, in every skin fold, and in-between your toes. Also, if you eat a lot of garlic, spices, hot peppers, onions, or fried foods, those smells show up in your skin—even with proper soapy crevice-scrubbing. YOU probably can't smell it. But she can. Unless you want the nickname *Curry Crotch, Onion Sac* or *Stinky Pete,* break out the soap and wash cloth! Don't get all obsessive and worried about it though. Just be aware that, when dating a new girl, the cleaner the better-especially initially.

For Mr. Half-Ass Shower, here is how it usually goes: a few hours after his meek shampoo-and-arm-pit shower, he is snuggling with his gorgeous dream girl on the couch—with hopes of fondling pretty boobies. He is starting to sweat—ever so slightly—and the moist heat starts penetrating his layers of dead skin and natural body hormones that have stockpiled due to his unaware showering habits. She catches a subtle whiff and BAM! Her subconscious *danger danger!* brain signals get triggered. She is turned off forever. She stands up with a look of horror on her face and announces, "Um… sorry! I need to get outta here!"… all probably without even knowing why. And being a guy—with his inferior olfactory senses and ignorance to how the female bio-chemistry works, he has NO clue why she pulled the plug out of the blue.

This is the mystery behind those perfectly awesome make out sessions that she suddenly STOPS for no apparent reason. You know the ones... when she asks you to get off of her and take her home— usually with tears in her eyes? If this has ever happened to you, think for a minute about how thoroughly you showered before your date? My guess is—not very well. If you got to the point that you were cuddling with her on the couch, then she did initially like you. Something else caused her to suddenly shut down. Ferociously furry backs and crusty toenails notwithstanding, that something was likely *inferior hygiene habits.*

Suddenly Stinky

Riddle: How does a woman tell her date that he smells bad?

Answer: She doesn't. She just disappears.

I remember well the day my sister, MARY—18 at the time, returned home early from a date with a guy she *really* liked: Pete. When he asked her out, she was over the moon for the entire week! She couldn't WAIT for Friday night to come—and had high hopes that she and Pete might actually have some potential. When the knock finally came, she turned and gave her sisters an exited and breathless look—one that only sisters understand to mean, "Don't wait up for me… and leave the back door unlocked so I can sneak in really late…" She floated out the door, and was *off!*

Yet… MARY returned just two hours after Pete picked her up. She came in, slammed the front door, and stormed back to our bedroom. She threw her purse down, took her shoes off, and threw them into the closet. She was obviously very upset. I asked her, "What's going on, Sis? And why are you home so early?"

She barked back, "Because that nasty creep needs to learn how to fucking shower!" I was shocked. My sister was normally so calm, and easygoing. I had never even heard her swear before. Hmmm...

"Is that all that's wrong?" I asked, a little concerned that something more serious went on that she wasn't telling me.

"YES! That is all. He reeks! We're sitting there, making out on the couch and I start smelling something so rank—it was like, ew. I couldn't figure out what it was, but then realized it was him!"

"Did he smell like moldy B.O.?" Mandy yelled from the front room. The Stinky Dumb-Fuck Club is looking for members!" *Bahahaha!* But MARY didn't laugh.

"No he smells like old sweat and gym socks mixed with... dirty tomatoes or something! So gross! He needs to learn how to fucking shower!" (Second use of the f-bomb. Holy crap! This was *serious!*)

Johnny, 12 at the time, heard the heated conversation and appeared in the doorway. "Hey! What do you mean, MARY, that he needs to learn how to shower? How hard can it be?"

MARY was MORE than happy to educate her little brother on the perils of subpar hygiene. "It means, Johnny, that when you take a shower, you don't just rinse off with a little soap under your armpits. You need to take the bar of soap and washcloth and scrub every single, solitary inch of yourself—TWICE! Because if you don't, you will stink like a dead animal when you start to sweat. And no girl will want to be near you. I can still smell him—all the way up to my BRAIN!" She stormed off to the bathroom to shower. "GROSS!" she said as went into the bathroom and slammed the door. Johnny and I just looked at each other, stunned at our sister's over-the-top fury. *(Note to Self: Soapy shower. Every single, solitary inch. Every crack & crevice. Every time. Head to toe. Twice. Got it.)*

Of course, MARY never told Pete why she didn't want to see him anymore. She just avoided his calls and completely stopped talking to him. Pete actually turned into QUITE the nuisance; he would call several times a day (our house phone; we didn't have cell phones back then), every day—for weeks. We would always tell him the same thing, "MARY isn't here."

"Can you tell her I called?"

"Yes, Pete."

Johnny was pretty confused by all this avoidance. He finally asked, "MARY, why don't you just be honest with that guy and tell him he stunk?"

"Because, Johnny. That's rude. You can't tell a guy he stinks. It will hurt his feelings."

"But it probably hurts his feelings that you keep ditching him."

"That's just how it is, Johnny."

That same day, Johnny answered the phone—after Pete's 6th attempt to reach MARY that day). "Um, hi Pete. This is MARY's brother."

"Yeah?"

"MARY doesn't want to talk to you because she said you stink and need to learn how to shower."

<dead silence on the other end >

"Later, Guy." Johnny hung up and looked into the faces of his horrified sisters—all of us ghost white and speechless.

He shrugged his shoulders. "At least he knows now and will stop calling." Leave it to Johnny.

Pete never did call again. It took a hyperactive 12 year old boy with budding empathy and big kahunas to set Stinky Pete straight. Via this phone call, Johnny's delivered his first dating-how-to tip—for one lonely, clueless, and sexually frustrated Pete. And, at the same time, learned another: *(Note to Self: A girl won't tell a guy why she doesn't like him. She'll just ignore him.)*

Note that a *Suddenly Stinky* guy doesn't just repel a girl; he usually triggers a visceral reaction—anything from annoyance to a deep rage within her. The reason for this is purely biological—again, as a female protection response.

Get this: as a woman, it is horribly invasive to have even a semi-stinky guy getting turned on and all over you. There is something about that combination that is just disgusting. The solution is beyond simple: soap, washcloth, scrubbing, respect, boundaries.

There are other possibilities for a girl suddenly getting turned off while making out, but none as common as the subtly smelly syndrome. Remember—she needs to get used to your natural smells... which is a very delicate process for females and requires you to initially present a body that is not swarming with them. But once she is emotionally attached (a.k.a. in love with you), meticulous crevice-scrubbing is not nearly as big of a deal. In fact, your natural smell will help her to stay bonded to you. Of course, this only applies to a certain extent... don't let yourself morph into smelly Neanderthal—even after you are in an established relationship. Not only is that disrespectful, you will turn her off when you try to initiate sex. Then you will be back on the single's scene, and back to meticulous crevice scrubbing all over again.

Let's review the concepts in this book so far:

- Don't try too hard to impress her. Just be yourself.

- Instead of bragging about yourself, talk to her about her.

- Shower very well—according to MARY's explicit directions.

- Wear clean clothes. No pulling shirts out of the wash hamper.

- Extremely easy on the cologne.

- Don't invade her bubble. Instead, let her come to you.

Taa Daaa! Which of these principles are too challenging for you to accomplish? NONE of them! You could master each of these NOW! Easy-peasy, man. Easy-peasy.

Other New Relationship Turn Offs

Beware! Here are a few other new-relationship turnoffs:

Forceful kisses: These usually involve the sticking your tongue down her throat and into her pancreas. (Be very cautious with tongue-heavy kisses with a new girl. Start soft and sweet... she will let you know if she wants more).

Incessant Texting: The cell phone has given the dating world a very bad, very difficult *perk*: instant access. This means that a guy who tends to obsessively think about a girl can do a lot of harm to not only his budding romantic relationships, but to his reputation, because he can just pick up his phone and bombard her with endless text messages. Very bad idea, Bro! She will feel cornered, pressured, trapped, and her survival instinct of shutting down and trying to get away from you will make sure your chances with her are over before they begin.

If you're feeling obsessed about seeing her or wondering if she likes you, chill. Give her a chance to return your text. Put your phone away. Especially, do not send her sexy pictures of you in your silky boxers. Remember? Women, unlike men, are generally **not** visually focused. You might get turned on by sexy pictures, but she probably won't. In fact, if you're not in an established relationship, a quality woman will think your pics are creepy. So no matter how sexy you think you look in your tighty-whities, do not – I repeat: do NOT send her those pics.

Brainless comments: These are often said out of nervousness, anxiety, or feeling of desperation—which can also result from *blue-ball syndrome*.

Awkward body postures, gestures, or movements: Guys, when you finally do get in bed with her—or even to the point of cuddling on the couch, you might be so excited and nervous that you lose all sense of logic. For instance, don't wrap your legs around her like a baby monkey. There is nothing remotely sexy about the *wrap my legs around her* move. That's a chick thing to do. She will feel smothered and creeped out.

Perpetual depression, negativity, or an *Oh poor me* attitude: a definite turn-off. Don't play the victim. Don't tell her about all the people who have screwed you over, stole from you or lied to you. She will probably listen and offer some support—all the while planning her escape… and never talk to you again.

Gnarly feet: If you have athlete's foot or toenails that look more like crustaceans from the bottom of the sea, she is going to get grossed out. So take care of these things without delay. See your doctor if necessary. Also, out-of-control calluses can look pretty nauseating to a female too. You can purchase a pumice stone from the health and beauty section of almost any drug store; use it on your calluses at least once a week in the shower, and then apply lotion. Don't get the lotion between your toes though; it can aggravate athlete's foot because lotion retains moisture.

But Really… Guys are Awesome

I know I'm hitting these points about turn offs pretty hard. But the truth is, guys are awesome. Guys are smart. Guys are dreamy. And you have it in you to get and keep any girl you want. You just need to realize and integrate that information in a way that will help you connect with your inner cool, your inner confident, your true and authentic inner YOU.

I want to impress upon you the importance of recognizing your true value. Guys are strong. Intelligent. Coordinated. Funny. Resilient. You can bag on each other with your friends all day long and are no worse for wear. (Girls can't handle heat like that.) You can build patios, work with wrought iron, catch a 90-mile-an-hour baseball, fix computers, and figure out stuff like a clogged pipe or a broken pool pump. Guys race cars, build motorcycles, work on complicated engines and never once wince at their dirty fingernails. Men are marvelous. But really, how many men recognize their inherent worth? Not from a conceited or egotistical standpoint (that's just fear) but from an innate recognition of their true value? I haven't met too many. And neither have the women I interviewed for this book. Yet, true self-confidence is the sexiest, most alluring quality a man can possess. It's worth it to start developing yours. How? Here are a few tips to get you started.

Start Appreciating Yourself

One of the biggest things that you can do to improve your confidence is simple: start appreciating yourself. Recognize what is right with you. Do this consistently, and confidence will naturally follow. A confident man is a sexy man. It doesn't matter what he looks like. On this same note, recognize the difference between *confident* and *conceited*.

Confidence comes from a deep appreciation for oneself. **Conceit** (meaning narcissistic or stuck up) comes from a hidden fear of unworthiness. This hidden fear prompts him to puff up his importance—and, yeah, it is a huge, HUGE turn-off to chicks.

For example, a truly confident man would never post a shirtless pic on his social media page, "Which one of you lucky girls wants to date this sexy mo fo?" Chances are, this guy would get a response from his lesbian friend, his derpy female cousin, and his mother saying, *That's right, honey. You are hot!*☺ Meanwhile, all his female friends are ignoring him, de-friending him, or marking themselves *in a relationship.* Why? Because fake confidence (a.k.a. *conceit* is one of the biggest romantic turn offs in the long, sad history of romantic turnoffs.)

Confidence is an energy that comes from within you. It can't be faked. Low self-esteem can't be covered up with money, nice clothes, cologne, a fancy phone, or expensive shoes. This is both good and bad news—depending on your viewpoint. But for the purposes of this book, it is very, very good news. It means that the thing that matters most to women—authentic confidence—won't cost you a thing to cultivate.

Kara and Joseph

Kara, 28, is an educated and beautiful woman with long strawberry blonde hair and dancing blue eyes. She was a runway model in her teens and early 20s, and left this profession after finishing college.

Kara relayed the following story to me over coffee one day, about how she met her husband. I felt it was important to include all of the details she gave me. This is translated verbatim from a recording, with the *umms, sooo's,* and excessive *ands* removed. The names have been changed... to protect the guilty. So in Kara's words:

I was working as a project manager for an online investment firm a few years ago. Upper management hired a computer programmer, Joseph—my now husband—to assist in our development of an online foreign exchange trading system; a lucrative but tricky business. I remember the day he walked into our office. At the risk of sounding heartless, well, I just didn't think he was very attractive. He looked just so... awkward and goofy. And he was tall and kinda skinny. He even had kind of a little belly—you know. He had a nice, white set of teeth though, and always smelled sooo good... so I did notice that. But the first time I ever saw him smile, well he was giving a talk at a staff meeting—I noticed something about him. I didn't know what it was, but he got my attention. He was genius. And very, very confident. Everything about him conveyed confidence. But he wasn't stuck up or anything. Not at all. He was just... confident; I don't know... his voice was deep, but not too loud. Just sure of himself. And he spoke with authority on the new program he was building for us. He was not particularly patient with us either, and answered our questions very matter-of-fact like. He wouldn't allow us to interrupt him and insisted we email him any questions. And there was simply nothing in his awareness that suggested he wasn't worth his weight in gold. But he didn't flaunt it either. He just...knew it. So one day when he was talking, I thought, "Damn! This guy's hot! Wait. No he's not! He's ugly!" I was so confused about my... being attracted to him... and then not thinking he was like, super good looking, or what I was used to dating. So many times he would pass my desk on his way in and wouldn't even look at me. Or he would just say, (flat) "good morning..." just like he said to everyone else. Then he would go straight to his office and work. And sometimes I would see him and think, "Why did I think he was hot? He's not. He's ugly."

And then he would show up to talk to us during our meeting, and he would smile. Or say something super intelligent. Or just radiate that amazing confidence that saturated every cell in his being. And I would be hooked again. Long story short, I fell for Joseph. Hard. I mean like—out of my of my mind, could barely think about anything else—hard. I was totally crazy about him, which was wrong on so many levels. Not only were we coworkers in a professional environment, at the time I was engaged to another guy, Gordon. But Gordon was a body builder, not like that's bad, but he was just so self-absorbed and full of himself. He was in a bunch of magazines and calendars and was a judge for body-building competitions and stuff. I was pretty much an accessory he could use to promote his crap and show off to his friends.

Gordon was also one of those stupid ex-football jocks who only talked about his glory days. And he was super controlling and would try to tell me what to wear and stuff. I can't believe I put up with him for two years.

Anyway, I was dolling myself up for work every morning just for that one moment when Joseph walked by my desk, and especially on Wednesday mornings for our staff meetings. But he never really noticed me. At least he never acted like it. That went on forever. So then I started thinking up questions for him just so I could go talk to him in his office. Half the time he would just say, "Can you email me? I'm in the middle of something..." God! It was torture.

I was dying to spend just one night with him. Well... that night eventually happened. And that's when I finally dumped Gordon for Joseph. It's a crazy story. Do you have time?

I nodded, more than eager to hear her hook-up story with the "ugly" man with the great brain and white teeth. Her story was completely validating what I already knew: when it comes to wooing women, confidence is better than muscles or looks. Kara sighed and took a sip of her coffee. "Are you going to use my real name in this book?"

"No."

"OK. Good. And don't use Joseph's name either.

"I'll change all the names. Don't worry. Go on…"

"Do you mind hearing the… you know… sex stuff?"

"Kara, I'm writing a book for men. I think we need the sex stuff."

"All right." She smiled smugly.

So… I was working late one day after work. Not that I needed to be. I was just there kinda waiting around for Joseph to leave so I could like, pretend I was leaving at the same time, so I could walk out with him. He always worked late. I saw his light shut off in his office down the hall. So I gathered my stuff to leave. He like—half waved at me and we ended up walking out together. He held the door while I set the alarm. When we got out to the parking lot, we saw that his front tire was flat. So he called his road side service thing. They told him that it would be at least two hours. So of course, I was ecstatic, but didn't let him know. If that would have happened to Gordon, the flat tire thing, he would have been yelling and swearing at the guy on the phone, and probably would have punched the hood of his car. But Joseph didn't even act upset. He just sat down on the curb and said, "You don't have to wait." And that was a big turn-on too, because Gordon always used to scare me by getting angry. Man—I hated that guy. I can't believe I wasted over two years of my life with him. But anyway, I told him (Joseph) that I didn't mind waiting, that I had a few questions about his (computer) program. I didn't really have any questions, but what the heck, right? So I asked him these bogus questions. We were just sitting on the curb there. It was a really nice evening, cloudy, and the sun was setting. All of the sudden he looked at me really intense like and said, "Kara, you're really pretty." Like he just noticed or something. My heart flopped into my throat. Honestly, I didn't even know that he knew my name. I tried to act like it was no big deal. But I was melting. So the tow truck guy called his cell phone at that exact minute (rolls her eyes) and said it would be at least three more hours. So Joseph asked if he could just tow his truck to the tire shop, and he would pick it up the next day. Then he hung up and asked if I would mind giving him a ride home and I said sure. He asked if he could take me to dinner for my trouble. Then Gordon started calling me a bunch of times. I didn't answer and ended up shutting off my phone. There was no way I was going to let that control freak ruin my chance with Joseph. So we ended up going to this little hole in the wall Italian place with these vinyl red-checker table cloths and wooden chairs. We had this wine that was probably from a box. But the whole thing was totally romantic. He was asking me questions about my family, my hobbies, and he actually seemed really interested. I never mentioned Gordon though. I tried to answer his questions casually, and asked him questions back, but all I was thinking about how bad I wanted to drag him to the ground and rip his clothes off. At this point, it had been over a year since he started working for our company, and I had been dreaming about him ever since.

He finally paid the bill. I told him I needed to stop in the bathroom. And I went in there and was trying to calm myself down. My heart was pounding super hard and I felt weak. I could tell he liked me too, at least a little. But unlike any guy I've ever dated, he was totally hands off. Interested, kind, and engaged in conversation, but not at all crowding my space. It was... awesome. And I knew for sure he wasn't a creeper. Anyway, I tried to like breathe deep and everything but nothing helped. I finally went back out there. When we got outside, it was dark and it was thundering, with some lightening off (waves her hand) you know-kinda far off in the distance. So we walked over to my car and watched the storm for a while. He was like... leaning on my car and I was standing kinda in front of him. Then I just reached my hand back to him and he grabbed it. Gently, but confidently. So I moved toward him a little. Finally, he hugged me like from behind, so my back was leaning on his chest. I couldn't even breathe—just him holding me like that... and I was so turned on that I could barely even stand up. And I could tell he was turned on he was too (laugh). But he still didn't do anything more than just hold me there. And we stood there and watched the clouds. Then thunder started really rolling, and the storm got closer, and it got windy, but we didn't move—just stood there for a long time, just watching the storm. Then he took one of his hands and brushed my hair to the side and started lightly kissing my neck and I was DYING... oh my God. And at that point, it was obvious that I liked him. So he finally turned me around and we started kissing like crazy. We stood out there, kissing, with lightning and thunder all around us. It started raining, but we stayed outside—kissing in the rain. (Long pause with "distant" look...) He finally opened up my car door and said, "Let's go." It was hilarious. No romantic, fancy words. Just, "Let's go." Gordon never used to open my car door... much less ever kiss me like that. Anyway, when Joseph got in on the passenger's side, he pulled me over onto his lap and kept kissing me and had his hands all over me—but he still didn't touch my boobs or... you know, privates, and didn't rub himself on me, or handle me in any creepy way. It was so crazy... to be... just taken in like that. With so much passion—and by someone I was so in love with too! It made me feel beautiful. I didn't need to set any boundaries. Because he wasn't crossing any. I literally had never had that happen with any guy. He was the first. I finally got back into the driver's seat and started driving, and my hair was tangled and all over the place. It was pouring rain, and I was a little nervous driving. We eventually got to his house, which was about 20 minutes away. Even though it was pouring outside, he got out of the car, walked around, opened the car door and grabbed my hand and said, "Come on." It wasn't a question. But, like everything he ever said, it was just a confident statement. "Come on." That was the extent of him trying to woo me with words. Because we got into his house and didn't even make it to the bedroom—I started ripping his soaking wet clothes off—just like I had been dying to do for months—and, finally, after it was obvious it was okay, he started unbuttoning my shirt. We had the craziest, best sex ever on his living room floor. But I did get rug burn on my spine. (laugh) I ended up spending the night and we had sex like a hundred times. Well... like four... And it was funny because the next morning I didn't have any clean clothes, and so he let me wash my clothes and I just wore them the next day. But no one said anything. We stopped for coffee at a little coffee shop not far from our work. We shared a raspberry Danish. We just had the most amazing few minutes over coffee—we were so connected! He ended up walking from the coffee shop to work so nobody knew I had given him a ride.

I called Gordon as soon as I got to my desk and left him a voicemail, telling him I didn't want to see him anymore and I was breaking up with him. He called me a bunch of times that day, but I wouldn't answer. He left voicemails, yelling at me and threatening me and acting like a complete jerk. But that was nothing new. But the weirdest thing was how Joseph just acted all... normal... at the office, like nothing had happened the night before. True, we weren't supposed to be dating each other. The only thing different was, when he walked by my desk and smiled at me and we locked eyes for a few seconds when he said, "Good morning." But then just went to his office. He sent me a text saying, "You're beautiful." I wrote back. "You are too." He wrote back, "Thanks for helping me last night with my flat tire." I wrote, "My pleasure!" He wrote, "So many responses I could text right now. Xo." I just sent a smiley back. Then he just stayed in his office and worked all day, never text me again or came by to chat or anything. So I still didn't know if he really liked-liked me, or if he was just, you know, not sure or whatever. He finally asked me out three days later, and we had another awesome, crazy night. Then acted all normal at work again. It was driving me nuts! I knew better than to chase him. So I just stayed to myself as much as I could. But eventually we started dating more and more, he would text me sexy things at work and stuff. But he still was totally into his work and acted like, well, he liked me, but liked work more… or something.

Oh, and I had to call the cops on Gordon, by the way, because he turned into a crazy ass hole. I ended up breaking my lease and staying at my brother's house until I found a new apartment. I changed my number and blocked him online. Thank God he never knew where I worked. He literally never once came to my work, or even asked where I worked. I used to be so angry because of it, but it turned out to be a blessing in disguise.

Also, I never told Joseph that I was engaged to someone else that first night we were together. I felt really guilty about it for a while. But Gordon and I had been engaged two years. And a few months before, I had taken the (engagement) ring off at his place when we were cooking one night. I used to do that a lot—and always put it in this glass bowl on his dresser. The same spot. But this time, when I went to put it back on, the ring was gone. Gordon swore he never saw it. He kept blaming me for losing it. But I know I left it in that bowl on his dresser. I'm pretty sure he pawned it. He was terrible with money. But at that point I didn't want to be engaged to him anymore anyway, so was glad I didn't need to wear the ring. And he kept dragging his feet on marrying me, and I didn't push it, because he was just... super controlling, always yelling and cutting me down and threatening me and stuff and blaming me for all of his problems.

I guess I didn't realize how miserable I was with Gordon until I met Joseph. So he and I had this super intense secret relationship for about six months, but people at the office were starting to suspect. So we finally out and told everyone at the Christmas party when we showed up together. But no one really cared, and we didn't get in trouble or anything. In fact, they all came to our wedding and pitched in and bought us a honeymoon to Hawaii. And you know, after being with Gordon for so long—it was... weird... like Joseph is so uninterested in his muscles, or how big his thighs were or how big his dick was. Joseph never yells at me or cuts me down. He always tells me how beautiful I am and how lucky he is to be with me. But he never gets suffocating or anything—he is just... easy going. He's always reading computer stuff and loves computer programming. He has about a hundred projects going all the time. And he lets me do my own thing, too. He never gets jealous or controlling. It's just... so nice. He's absolutely my best friend.

"So how did he propose?" I asked.

Oh, like a year later, he took me to dinner at that same hole-in-the-wall Italian restaurant. He had the waiter put my ring on top of my dessert, and when I saw it, he got on one knee and proposed. Nothing over the top crazy, but nothing he does ever is!"

Let's Hit Pause and Review

- By societal standards, Joseph was physically <u>un</u>attractive

- He was vested in his own work and interests—and not the pursuit of women

- He was confident to his core

- He was not egotistical or conceited

- He got the attention of Kara, a brilliant, beautiful woman

- He paid no attention to her for the first two months they worked together

- She developed a massive crush on him

- Joseph and Kara ended up serendipitously having sex in a frenzy one night—that she mostly initiated

- She dumped her body-builder, calendar-quality jock fiancé for an "ugly computer nerd"

- When they first connected, Joseph kissed Kara passionately, but remained respectful of Kara's body and boundaries

- Joseph's calm and respectful actions helped Kara feel safe and relaxed around him

- Joseph is now married to the woman of his dreams

By the way, of all the women I interviewed for this book, a whopping 90% of them said that they had fallen hard for a man whom they initially considered unattractive.

Score Point: Attraction has very little to do with your physical appearance. It's all about confidence. Not conceit—as in what Gordon displayed, but CONFIDENCE—as in what Joseph displayed.

Now boys, what do you think would have happened if Joseph had made it obvious that he noticed Kara, the beautiful former runway model, as soon as he started working at the office? What if he had started pursuing her in those first few days? What if he bugged her at work and was constantly hanging out at her desk? What if he stopped being interested in his computer programming career, did a half-ass job at work, and then spent the rest of his time trying to get in Kara's pants? What if he would have ranted and raged over his flat tire that night while Kara stood by timidly? What if he had then asked her out, and provided she even accepted his date, showed up for the date with roses, a squeaky clean car, and shiny black patent-leather shoes? Then consistently invaded her space and body in trying to push intimacy? I don't think I need to spell this out for you—he would have been dissed by her and never given a second look. She would have talked to her friends about the "creepy new programmer" at her office and rolled her eyes every morning when he walked by her desk and said hello. Sad but true. Females are like that. But after she was hooked on him? Roses and nice dinners melted her further. Lastly, he showed up fully, but never lost himself to her and the relationship.

Should You Even Ask a Girl Out Then?

Obviously—yes! Just follow the guidelines here. This book is in no way suggesting that you should never ask a girl on a date. Of course you should! In fact, the man must be the pursuer in the relationship. Otherwise, if she pursues you, the passion will quickly fizzle. And you do need to pay her some attention, behave like a gentleman, and show her you are at least semi-interested. But for goodness sake, honor yourself first. If you truly feel compelled to bring her flowers, instead of buying her a whole bouquet of roses, buy her a single rose. But before buying even a single flower, examine your reasons for doing so. Do you think you need to "prove" what a good guy you are? Do you think she won't like you just as you are? Do you think flowers will increase your chances of her liking you? None of these are good reasons to bring her flowers. But if you just love to see her smile and you want to surprise her, then, well, these are good reasons. Just don't delude yourself into thinking that your flowers will help her become more attracted to you—especially if you give them for the wrong reasons. Energy, my good man. It's all about your core and confident energy.

Keeping Your Green

While wining and dining are basic parts of the dating process, it is important that you do not spend money you don't have. Don't spring for a meal you can't afford. Don't take her to the most expensive restaurant in your city. Take her to a nice place, yes. But one you can afford. Be a gentleman. Open the door (including the car door) for her, pull out her chair, and use your manners. No talking with your mouth full, chewing with your mouth open, or belching at the table.

Absolutely do not delude yourself into thinking that a girl will fall for you if you spend $200 on dinner with her. No dinner has ever made any woman fall for a man. It's your confidence (but not arrogance), your respect (but not desperation) and your pleasant (but not too eager to please) attitudes—borne from true confidence—a very attractive energy—that ultimately matter to the woman in question.

If you aren't sure how a girl really feels about you and you want to find out, start out casually. "Wanna grab some coffee?" or "Are you going to Jacob's party this weekend?" are much easier questions than, "Do you want to have dinner on Saturday night?" If she likes you, she will go to coffee with you. If she doesn't accept the coffee invite, the rejection is minor, and you will recover quickly. Then you can save your Saturday night for a different girl or a night with the guys. And if things seem to go well on your coffee date, THEN you can ask her to dinner later in the week. This way you keep your dignity AND your money. But with all that being said, you must take some risks. The man MUST pursue a woman. This is an energetic principle. And waiting for the stars to align into ideal circumstances (as in the case with Kara and Joseph) could leave you waiting forever.

Quick Ways to Build Confidence

Develop Skills: The first suggestion I have for confidence-building is this: develop a skill that really interests you. Become the expert at something! Preferably, develop a skill that is very exciting to you and lights your fire. Allow that hobby to take up your extra time... or the time you are currently using to pine away after girls. This will exponentially boost not only your confidence, but how attractive you are to women. And your sudden energetic elusiveness will probably intrigue her.

Get Smart: My second suggestion: get educated. If you're in school—no matter what level—strive for excellent grades. This isn't a pep talk to try to get you to do—whatever. It's a way for you to demonstrate that you love and respect yourself—enough to work hard and stay focused on your own goals. Even if you're in a trade that doesn't require college, take some classes or pursue a certification that gives you a really solid niche. Not only will this radically boost your confidence, she will notice that you strive for excellence in your life. Chicks dig this.

Invest in yourself: Invest in yourself and quit looking to women to make you feel good about yourself. As Napoleon Dynamite put it, "Girls only want guys who have good skills!" And in a very real way this is true. Actually, the secret ingredient isn't really the skill, but the confidence that comes from becoming an expert on something. Additionally, pursuing hobbies and interests will take up your time, making you ultimately less available—a.k.a.: more attractive!

Become more interested in your own life than in hers. Guys that do nothing but pursue women come across as desperate. Women aren't attracted to men who don't have much of a life! In essence, put dating second, and your own life first. Always.

Do what ever you can do to become really invested in your own life. You don't need a girlfriend to be happy. You need to get happy first! Because girls love to be around confident, happy guys who don't need them.

This doesn't mean slapping on a smile when you feel pissed off or lonely. It means doing the things that you really like doing. Play basketball in the park. Build your brick grill or outdoor kitchen. Get involved in a creative project. Meet some friends to watch a game at the sports bar. Work on your bronco that's been sitting in the garage for five years. Go work out at the gym or spend the evening with your brother playing an online video game. Take up a boxing class or go back to college. And don't be looking at your phone every five minutes to see if she has called or text you. That's not a good energy; if you do, you will feel desperate on the phone with her when you finally do talk to her.

Frankie Smith: the Energetic Bully

Desperation kills attraction. Never has this been more evident than with one **very** good looking young man I knew in high school: Frankie Smith.

Frankie Smith (not his real name, of course) was a year younger than me. Frankie was *extremely* good looking, fairly intelligent, and, really, a pretty decent guy. I always liked Frankie in high school—not as a boyfriend, but just because he was such a good guy. He came from a good home, always played sports, and he was really cool and nice to everyone. At least… this is how I remembered him in high school. He stood about 6'2 with green eyes and gorgeous, thick light-brown hair. He could have modeled for the cover of a GQ magazine—he was that sexy-beautiful. Hawt... hawt... HAWT! Until he ruined it all with ignorance... and desperation for a girlfriend kicked in—long about junior year.

Sadly, in spite of his physical gifts and hotness factors, Frankie had NO idea how to relate to women. In his junior year; Frankie quit the football team so that he could "spend more time with his new girlfriend." (FAIL!) One month later, she left him for the varsity running-back. Of course, Frankie's big mistake was giving up his own passions and interests (football) and making his whole life about her. A big no-no—and it cost him big-time. She wasn't *more* attracted to him when he started spending extra time with her. She was *far less* attracted to him. Because he was WAAAYYY too available. That, and he wasn't living his own life anymore—he was trying to live hers. He duped himself into believing that she was his source of happiness. *<*insert crash and burn sound here*>*

Sadly, Frankie really went down the romantic shitter after high school. Sadder still: Frankie had zero skills when it came to relating to women. First of all, Frankie decided that, for whatever reason, skin-tight jeans were a jolly-good idea—I guess to show off the size of his pecker… which, admittedly, was... well, impressive... at least from what I could tell from his omnipresent and conspicuous bulge. In spite of the fact that Frankie subscribed to Captain Tripod Monthly, his efforts to show off his manhood came across as completely pathetic. Further, to make sure that all could enjoy his expertly sculpted chest, arm, and back muscles—again—quite impressive—Frankie wore skin-tight tee shirts to compliment his Stranglers...er ... I mean Wranglers. He completed his outfit with pointy-toed yellow cowboy boots that made entirely too much noise when he walked. His *thunk-click... thunk-click* could be heard for blocks—which was extremely counter-productive in his efforts to meet and bed women—mainly because we could all hear him coming from two blocks away—and would all be in hiding by the time he rounded the corner.

Frankie's appearance screamed, "Hey! Look at me! *(thunk-click... thunk-click...)* You want some of this? *(thunk-click... thunk-click...)* This could be your lucky day!" *(thunk-click... thunk-click...)*

Frankie *thunk-clicked* all over our neighborhood, looking for chicks. He *thunked* up the streets, and *clicked* down the alleys. He *thunk-clicked* his way in and out of the convenience store, arcade, and the pizza parlor. Sadly for Frankie, the only thing ever waiting for him around the corner was the lonely echo of his *thunk-clicking* footware... his *thunck-clicking* YELLOW footware... which possessed one (and only one) valuable ability to momentarily take the attention off of his grotesque skin-tight attire.

Poor Frankie. No girl cometh. Ever.

One day, about a year after high-school, I had the unfortunate experience of running into Frankie at the neighborhood convenience store—which is when I first realized that he seriously had a bubble off center. I remembered him from high school as a good guy, and I gave a friendly "hello!" Though a little taken aback with his new macho-guise... and his bright yellow cowboy boots (I never did get that angle...) it was obvious that I was happy to see him. Suddenly, his whole energy shifted—and he started energetically coming on to me really strong. He stood too close to me, asked for my phone number, and asked if he could take me to dinner. It was suffocating. I made up a bogus story that I was engaged and my fiancé was a jealous cage fighter who was always looking for someone to pummel. But Frankie didn't care. He persisted with his desperate efforts to convince me to go out with him; he stood even closer to me, and kept trying to put his hands on me. His actions repulsed me and I couldn't get away from him fast enough. He followed me out of the store, begging me to go to the movies with him; I got in my car, slammed the door, backed out and squealed out of the parking lot. I didn't even buy the stuff I went to the store for in the first place. *Oh my HELL! What a psychotic weirdo!!* I was annoyed, to say the least, and tried to shake off his creep vibe all the way home. But... at his core, Frankie wasn't a creep. He just had no self-awareness or self-love, and became an energetic vampire around any potential dating partner.

When I got home, I was still heebie-jeebied out; I told my sister what happened. Ashley looked at me, disgusted. "Oh, you mean Frankie Smith, that guy who quit the football team for that bitchy girl? He's a goon! I saw him at Heidi's party last Friday, and he wouldn't leave me alone! I had to totally ditch him!" A conversation ensued about Frankie's wardrobe—including his footwear, and my sister and I had a good laugh.

Of course, not ten feet away, John was sitting, taking it all in. *(Note to Self: Loose, relaxed clothes... hang back... hands off... stay out of her bubble... chill. Return yellow cowboy boots to Boot Barn...)*

At the time, I was working at a cosmetics counter in a department store. A month after my hellish Frankie run-in at the convenience store, I heard an eerily familiar *thunk-click... thunk-click...* echoing through the mall. The footsteps quickened. My heart pounded. Could it be…? The *thunk-clicks* were rapidly approaching the cosmetics department! *<insert sound bite from Psycho here/>* I saw him walk into the store, heading straight for my counter! I gasped and ducked, and prayed for my life. I was sweating. I stayed, crouched behind the counter, with my extremely confused customer waiting patiently… Several grueling, *thunk-clicking* minutes passed.

Suddenly, the *thunk-clicks* ceased. As our department was carpeted, I had no audible signal where Frankie might be in our department. I peered up over the counter top. No Frankie Smith in sight. *Whew!* I stood up and continued the makeover I was doing. "Creepy-Ass Weirdo alert!" I said to my client.

"Oh!" She nodded. "I get it, Girl!"

See guys? Women get it. There are no exceptions. Even if you are a physically gifted, super hot, sexy dude like Frankie was underneath it all, you can blow it by coming on like a love-sick rhinoceros.

You can't be a needy, sex-starved, hopeless-romantic and expect girls to feel safe around you! Of course, as always, there are a few… exceptions to this rule, but those usually involve you radically lowering your standards. Actually, this is the case with Frankie that day. Here's what happened. About twenty minutes after Frankie disappeared, Phyllis, a kindhearted, sweet, and middle-aged lady who worked at the fragrance counter on the other side of the department—married, with four kids, and a bit on the chunky-and-frumpy side—walked up to my counter. "Oh my gosh! You're never gonna guess what just happened!"

"What?" I asked. "Do tell!"

"This really hot guy came up to the fragrance counter and started talking to me! He said, 'You know, you're really good lookin'! We need to hang out!' I couldn't believe he was talking to me! Did you see him? He was talking to me for like 20 minutes, begging me to go out with him. He was tall with thick brown hair with a tight white tee-shirt with big, huge muscles! Of course, I'm married, so I turned him down flat. But he wanted me to go to have lunch and then go out to his car with him! He wouldn't leave me alone until Bill (the floor manager) walked up to him and made him leave. Can you believe it?"

"Phyllis—that's... awesome!" I stifled a laugh and forced it into a broad smile.

"Wow! I guess I still got it!" She swaggered away with a beaming gleam in her eye.

"Of course you've still got it, Girlfriend!" I said with as much enthusiasm as possible. *(Oy... awkward! Biting tongue...)*

"Thanks!" She bellowed back, with her still beaming swagger. She didn't stop smiling for the rest of the day. It was actually very sweet.

I never did tell her that the guy who was wooing her was Frankie Smith, the *Thunk-Clicking Bandit of the West* who came onto anything with eye-lashes and a V.

Let's Hit Pause and Review

- Frankie Smith was physically GOR-geous.

- He was tall, chiseled, handsome and muscular.

- He was evidently hung like a feral water buffalo.

- He had all the physical qualities that women allegedly want.

- He couldn't get a girl to talk to him for nothin'... save a pudgy, middle aged married woman working the department store fragrance counter. And even she turned him down flat.

Let's look at this very carefully. What exactly was missing from Frankie's romantic-skill set?

- Self-Awareness

- Authentic confidence

- An understanding of female attraction principles

- An interest in his own life

- Jeans that didn't cut off the circulation to his balls

- Quiet, non-yellow, non thunk-clicking footwear

Always practice good high jean

Frankie Smith was physically gifted, yet completely socially clueless. Regrettably, I do not know the model, the original photographer or source of this picture... but it's a perfect depiction of Frankie Smith!

It's All Fixable!

If you notice, every single social and romantic snafu on Frankie's list here is quickly and completely fixable—with just a little awareness.

When it came to dating, Frankie was waaaayyyy too attached to the outcome, and met every woman with his suffocating, desperate expectations and neediness. Sadly, each rejection chipped away at his self-esteem. He probably started doubting how good looking he was and developed the perception that he was a *loser*.

NONE of this was true, of course. His problem was, quite simply, his inability to create any semblance of life outside of his desperate desire for a girlfriend. My educated guess is that Frankie ended up with a chick he met at a dive bar; she got pregnant in a drunken stupor... and they are living out their days in a double-wide, screaming at each other and chasing after seven squallerin' brats: *(thunk-click... "Get over here, you little thug!" (thunk-click... thunk-click...) "Clean up 'dem funyons!" (thunk-click... thunk-click..) "Who left dis corn dog on da couch?!! (thunk-click... thunk-click...) "Don't you smart back to me, boy! (thunk-click... thunk-click...) "Who let the chicken out of its coop?" (thunk-click... thunk-click...) You know we don't want Ol' Man Crapple catchin' him for dinner!" (thunk-click... thunk-click...) "Damn kids don't think..." (thunk-click... thunk-click...) "Sweetheart, wher'd you put the duct tape?" (thunk-click... thunk-click...) "Oh, hot dayumm, Darlin'! Yer lookin' fine in dem rollers and slippers!" (thunk-click... thunk-click...) "Get* *over here and love on yer big, strong, handsome home boy" (thunk-click... thunk-click...) *she runs and hides...**

Poor Frankie. Poor, clueless, thunk-clicking Frankie.

Building Confidence: Talking to New Girls

Now that we are clear in the hygiene, attire, confidence, and behavior departments, here are a few ideas that will help you build confidence in talking to girls... and getting to that first date. With all of these tips, keep in mind how important it is to respect a woman's personal space. In other words—don't be a Frankie Smith!

Random Compliments

Jim, 24, explains the random compliments technique this way: "Go out to a busy place, like the mall or a bar with a buddy. Take turns walking up to girls and giving them random compliments and then just walking away. If you are really intimidated, start out with girls who aren't very attractive, and give compliments like, 'I just want to tell you that you have beautiful hair' or 'Just so you know, you have gorgeous eyes.' Smile at her, then walk away and expect nothing. Make sure your compliment is genuine. Everyone has good qualities. So find those qualities and use those. Do this over and over again with different girls until you get used to talking to the opposite sex. You will feel nervous at first, trying to talk to a girl, even one who isn't super sexy. But think of it this way: not only will you probably make her day, you will get more and more confident talking to girls. Then try it with prettier girls. The trick is to walk away afterwards with no expectations. Whatever you do though, don't make your comments sexual or perverted. Keep a respectable distance. And don't touch her. Avoid complimenting her rack or her ass. Because you might get slapped. Even lips can be taboo. It depends how you say it."

Cute Puppy!

Guys, I know you don't get this. But girls love cute, fluffy, cuddly animals, kids, babies, even plush toys. They don't necessarily want these qualities in their boyfriends. But! You can capitalize on this tendency and have it work in your favor.

Paul admits to being really shy when it comes to talking to girls, and especially has trouble 'breaking the ice' with total strangers. But he does have one way of getting girls to talk to him without much effort. "My friend and I sometimes take my mom's friendly Pomeranian, Lucy, to the busy strip mall to walk around. Almost every girl who walks by looks at her and says, "Awww! How cute!" and stops to pet her. Lucy gets really excited and starts wagging her tail like crazy, kissing them, and sometimes rolls over on her back. Then the girl usually says, "She's so adorable! What's her name?" or "How old is she?" And I answer her questions. If she seems like a girl I want to date I will say, 'She (my dog) really likes you! Can I take a picture of you holding her?' She will usually say 'yes.' Then I say, 'Great pic! I'll send it to you. What's your number?' I send it to her and say, 'What's your name so I can put it in my phone?' Then I say, 'Okay. Got it. I'm Paul. Well, have a great rest of your day!' And smile and just walk away. Then I wait for her to text me. Then I know she likes me too. Works like a charm. (Paul is 17. Smart kid!)

20 Seconds of Confidence

Vince, 26, gives the "20 Seconds of Confidence" advice to guys: "Too many guys are scared of rejection. You gotta get over that. Anybody can get confident for 20 seconds. Here's what to do: when you see a girl you want to ask out, tell yourself that you are the most confident, best looking, most awesome guy on the planet. Stand up straight and feel it in your gut. Tell yourself that no matter what her response is, it doesn't matter, because you are just practicing being confident. But don't be pushy or loud or obnoxious, because girls hate that. In fact, talk kinda quiet and laid back. Just walk up and smile and say, 'Hi! Sorry for just walking up like this, but you are really pretty. Do you wanna go out sometime?' Usually they say 'no' and then you just say, 'Okay, just thought I'd ask. Have a good day!' Keep smiling and walk away. I mean... who cares? It's just 20 seconds of your life that you get to practice being confident and get immune to rejection. And if you're nice like that, sometimes they will say, 'Wait, hold on a sec...' and come over to talk to you and want to go out with you anyway. And sometimes, they say yes right away and will give you their number. I've gotten six girlfriends this way. But I've probably asked over 200 girls, too."

Personal Space, Anyone?

Let's talk a bit more about her personal space bubble. By now you know: no groping, grabbing, standing too close, no wrapping your legs around her while making out, no invading her bubble. I've made these principles very clear, and you can absolutely execute each and every one of them. But there are going to be a few of you who test these rules or think they don't apply to you—for whatever reason. Don't be a dumbass, Dude. They do apply to you.

Reality check: it does matter, especially with high quality women. Until a girl enters YOUR bubble, and clearly shows you that she wants to be close to you, any efforts you make to close the gap too quickly will blow up in your face. Even if a girl really, really likes you, you will ruin your chances if you come on to her in a smothering, needy way. Show her you are interested, yes, but let her come to you first. Don't test this boundary. Just... don't.

You have no idea how difficult it is, as a female, to get a clueless, over-eager, horny *thunk-clicker* out of your personal space. It's a total, all-encompassing energetic assault. It's far better to keep a bit of distance (while staying kind and respectful—don't get all distant and cold here...) than it is to "test" to see how close she will let you get to her before pushing you away.

If you enter her bubble too early in the relationship, before she feels comfortable with you—or, really, before she enters your bubble— her guard will come up big time. She will instantly be turned off, and when she does finally get free from your clueless pawing, panting, and groaning and moaning, she will run for the hills, and never look back.

Buddy, listen. It's natural for women to seek safety in men. A woman wants to know that you would protect her from the creeps and dangers of the world—not in a possessive, jealous kind of way, but in a manly, strong, and confident kind of way. So whatever you do, don't act in a way that remotely suggests that you are one of the creeps or dangers of the world.

Let's go over a few more scenarios. When it comes to hugging her— especially the first few times—make your hugs heart-felt, strong, but fairly brief, with NO strong-holds. She should be able to disengage from your hugs easily. And be sure to TAKE HER CUES. If she is trying to pull away from you, let her go. Immediately. Unless it's been established (later in the relationship) that she likes to "play" this way. Some girls do. But at this point, **assume nothing of the sort.**

CAW! CAW! The Creepy-Ass-Weirdo!

Almost any perfectly normal, nice-looking, intelligent guy can come across as a Creepy-Ass-Weirdo (CAW!) if he behaves poorly or follows runaway hormonal impulses. The best CAW prevention is awareness—and knowing what is and is not acceptable behavior with a new dating prospect.

I once had a blind date with a guy—I'll call him Walt. My friend assured me that he was a really nice guy—that he was respectful and intelligent. I hesitantly accepted the date, more so because of my friend's enthusiasm than my own. I mean... it's one date. What could go wrong? When Walt greeted me in the restaurant lobby, he reached out to give me a hug. Not too terribly concerning... but generally, let her reach out to hug you first. I gave him a brief A-frame hug. At least, that was my intention; I released my side of the hug right away, but Walt just hung on, and hung on, and hung on—and wouldn't let me go—as if he never had a hug from a woman before. WTF? Ew! Total turn off. Guys, this has CREEPY ASS WEIRDO (CAW!) written all over it. (CAWWW!! CAWWW!!) My thoughts? Let me go, you whacko dip-shit. NOT a good way to begin a first date.

I was more than annoyed. A definite strike one. There were other cardinal first-date sins committed that night, such as him spilling to me about his horrific money troubles, his crushing bouts of depression, and (OYE! Nooo...) that he was "looking for a woman who can help fix his life and tell him to snap out of it when he starts going down a negative emotional path." Oh yay! Where do I sign up for that fun and enchanting life??!!! He also talked with food in his mouth and spit little specks of food all over the table, killing my appetite. He had a few redeeming qualities; he was very intelligent, and (parts of) the conversation were interesting. At the end of the date, he walked me to my car. I had no intention of hugging or kissing him. (Take a cue from her body language—if she doesn't reach for you, she doesn't want a hug. If she doesn't put her face by yours, she is not interested in a kiss.) But before I got in my car, Walt literally grabbed my face and forced a kiss on me. When I resisted, pushing him away, he said, "Come on… just one little kiss…" (CAWWW! CAWWW!) I was completely disgusted, felt violated, and couldn't get away from him fast enough.

Walt had many fatal dating flaws. But by far, the worst first-date sins he pulled that night was his assault on my personal space. Like most women, the CAW factor was an absolute deal breaker for me. I thought, "If this is how he acts on a first date and in public, I sure wouldn't ever be safe should I ever be alone with him!"

Walt made his own agendas far more important than mine. He was downright ignorant of my own wishes and boundaries. The next day, he sent me an apology via email, stating, *sorry about the kiss. That was selfish on my part.*

While I appreciated the apology, it was just too late. Walt had already shown his true colors. He let his desperate need for affection ruin any chance of me ever wanting to go out with him again. Ever, ever, EVER!

I have turned down his subsequent offers from him since then to get together—much to his disappointment and bewilderment. Because from his perspective, the date went very well. We both had a GREAT time, and the chemistry between us was AMAZING, and we are meant to be, forever and ever. Um… what's the phrase I'm looking for here? "NOT!" And he wonders why he's been single for over ten years. CAWWW!

Your Mind Can Mess with You

This brings me to another important point: if you have been lonely for a while, be aware that your mind can mess with you while you are with a woman—especially a woman you really like. You will believe that the chemistry between you two is stronger than it really is. You will assume that she is absolutely as interested in having sex with you as you are with her. So if you are silently planning on getting lucky after the date, give yourself a reality check. She may not be on that same page. She is still sizing you up, wondering if you are who you say you are: wondering if you're a grumpy bear, an alcoholic, workaholic, sexaholic, dorkaholic. Are you perverted? Integral? Fun? Creative? Self-reliant? Deep-thinker? Arrogant? Tall-tale-teller? Empathic? Intuitive? Selfish? Spiritual? Religious? A bible-beater? A swinger? Bi-sexual? Closet homo-sexual? Do you have kids? Are you a good dad? Could you have kids you don't know about? Are you psychopathic? Narcissistic? Schizophrenic? Bi-Polar? Angry? A liar? Scheming? A womanizer? Do you have a sense of entitlement? Do you take good care of your pets? Are you neat? A slob? Integral? Reasonable? Self-reliant? Cyber-stalker? Sociopath?

Chances are, you're a sweetheart and an awesome guy, and would make an excellent boyfriend. But since she still knows very little about you, you could very easily blow it by following overeager hormonal impulses—**even if she thinks she is starting to like you.**

On a first date, it is far better to give far less affection, and let her come to you (because if she is interested, she will) than it is to try to see how far you can get with her in the parking lot—and probably turn her off forever. In fact, this is just another version of the Frankie Smith thunk-clicking moron we discussed in our last chapter. So, if she reaches for you first, simply reciprocate with a genuine, heartfelt, and easy hug goodnight.v(Don't be soft or wimpy about it... just genuinely hug her, from the heart!) This way, she won't feel threatened and will drop her guard around you the next time you two are together. And if the conversation was engaging, fun, and enjoyable... TAA-DAAA! She's definitely looking forward to date number two.

Score Point: Show some class. Don't strong-arm affection. Let her come your way!

Instead of overreacting when your dream girl starts paying attention to you, train yourself to do the following:

Take a deeeep breath.

Systematically relax all of your muscles, starting at the top of your head and working your way down your body.

Take another deeeep breath.

Silently repeat to yourself, *chill... chill... chill... personal space... personal space... personal space... let her come to me.*

Smile.

Repeat.

You are an awesome, respectable, desirable man—with all the tickets for attracting and dating your dream girl. The next time you connect with a girl, just try my suggestions here. Allow her to admire you from a distance. Let her come close and run her fingers over your textured paint... and dream about what it might be like to take you home.

H.a.n.g. b.a.c.k. C.h.i.l.l. B.r.e.a.t.h.e. L.e.t. h.e.r c.o.m.e. t.o. m.e.

Tons of girls would love to date you. You just don't get it, because you might not believe it's this simple. The only difference between you and the guys getting all the chicks is how they behave and the energy they exude. This is dictated by their level of self-love, confidence, personal joy, and their level of trust in letting the process unfold.

Dance Floor FAIL!

Let's take these same concepts of personal space and apply them in the night club. Obviously, things are little looser, more relaxed, more playful in this environment. People are a little tipsy and tend to take more romantic risks. But do not—I repeat—do NOT lose sight of everything you've learned in this book so far just because you are suddenly swimming in eye candy, alcohol, and raging hormones. The same principles apply: hands to yourself. Out of her bubble. Behave like a gentleman. This will intrigue her, because every other hairy-scary dude is trying to cop a feel and treating her like his next manly conquest (CAW!)

The concept of respectful boundaries carries over to the dance floor. One of the worst things a guy can do is be an overzealous, hormonally charged dance partner who sees dancing with a girl as an opportunity to rub himself all over her. This happened to me and my sisters *way* too many times to count. (CAWWW!) And never once did any one of us think, "Oh, yay! A creepy-ass-weirdo is dancing with me! I hope he asks me for my phone number!" It was more like, "Hey dumbass! You're in my bubble!" *(Note to Self: When dancing, back up. She will come your way if she wants to.)*

The next time you decide to go clubbing and start dancing up on her, pay attention. Unless she is slobbering drunk or strung out of her mind (and you don't want that girl anyway) OR is really into you, she is probably trying to subtly push you away. Most girls aren't very good at setting healthy boundaries or speaking their mind. Most women drop subtle clues and expect guys to "get it." Sadly, most guys don't. If she is turning away, pushing you back with her hands, or physically backing away from you, this isn't a sign for you to *try harder.* You are in her bubble, dude. Just back up.

Read & Heed Her Body Language

Some men misinterpret her resistance on the dance floor as a sort of cat-and-mouse game. They completely miss her subtle clues and act like a *CAWWW!* So after you've used her as an effectual pecker primer, pay particular attention to the rest of the night and how she behaves towards you. Because chances are, she is going to ditch any guy who invaded her space on the dance floor. And you, being completely oblivious to the fact that girls just don't like being treated like vertical blow-up dolls, have an internal conversation with yourself that goes something like this: *Oh, hell… what's wrong with me? Every girl I like can't stand me! She must think I'm ugly. Maybe I need to suck in my gut. Maybe I need better shoes. I knew I shouldn't have worn this stupid shirt! Maybe I need to get hair plugs. I KNEW I shouldn't have tucked my pecker under. She probably couldn't feel it when we were grinding. Great, now she thinks I have a little dick. Oh my God! What if she thinks I have a little dick? I'll never get a girlfriend! Oh- hey! There's a cute girl! I think I'll go ask her to dance… maybe she will like me. Oh, I hope I hope!*

Get off the crazy train, Baryshnikov. You are dancing in her bubble. That's all. There is absolutely nothing wrong with you. Just back up.

You are an interesting and attractive man with awesome qualities, I promise you. But those qualities may be getting drown-out if you possess an over-eager drive for female attention and body contact. No woman will ever take the time to truly get to know a man who is *shoving his painting in her face.* But if he would just leave it on the wall of the gallery in all its splendor, she would be drawn to the painting by sheer intrigue. This is easy to fix, isn't it?

Now, if she starts dancing up on you, and she is clearly looking for the same, it's fine to reciprocate. But less is more here—so start out low-key, and always let her dictate the amount of body contact and distance between you. You'll be one of the few guys that do this, and she will appreciate it.

A Few Random New Dating Guidelines

1) Just because a girl is nice to you, doesn't mean that she is thinking about getting in bed with you. Assume nothing! When it comes to romance and affection, let her come to you.

2) Keep your hands to yourself. There are no exceptions to this rule.

3) Don't give her any "I want to hump your brains out" stares. You will scare her off.

4) If all you think about is dating, getting laid, or finding a woman to complete your life, you probably aren't getting any. If you are getting any, it's not from women you really want. Shift mental gears—back onto your own life.

5) Comparing yourself to other men is a waste of time and energy. It changes nothing and either makes you arrogant or depressed—depending on if you think you are better off or worse off than your compare-ees.

6) It doesn't matter how old you are; these principles apply whether you are 15, 25, 55 or 95.

Cruisin' for (an Ego) Bruisin'

Many years after my awful Frankie Smith experience, I went on a tropical cruise. After dinner one night, I met a fascinating gentleman named Lance. Lance had an unusual career; he hand-crafted marionette puppets and sold them to theatres around the world. He was well-spoken, intelligent, and beyond interesting. I found him extremely attractive. I asked him what type of work he did. He told me about his puppet business.

One of the most interesting puppets he told me about was a comical one-eyed monster puppet that was set to debut in a theater in London next month. (Coool!) I imagined Lance would be a creative, fun, and interesting person to get to know, and possibly have a shipboard romance with. We talked for about ten minutes, and (ooohhh boy)...

I was *really* interested. He finally said, "You and your husband (pointed to a man standing next to me—who was just a friend) should come up to my room. I'm on the balcony. I can show you my website and videos of my puppets."

"Oh…" I gestured towards my friend. "He and I aren't married or together. But, I would love to see your work."

Lance's Critical Mistake

Lance's *critical mistake* came down to one defining moment. After I told Lance I wasn't married or with to the man standing next to me, his whole energy shifted. It literally took less than three seconds for me to feel it—and lose any and all desire to get to know him any further. Lance started gazing at me like a cheetah getting ready to pounce on his prey. I could literally feel his energy "latch on" to me and start to suck the life out of me. I was instantly turned off, and, in truth, a little creeped out. I high-tailed it out of there as fast as I could. I avoided making eye-contact with him for the rest of the cruise. I had absolutely no more interest in him or his one-eyed puppet. And I guarantee you, if I were to point out his shift in his energy and how it scared me off, he would have NO clue what I was even talking about. He would have gone over the whole discussion in his mind several times, and concluded that I was just misconstruing details, or that he was just unattractive. Neither conclusion would be true, of course. He just became overeager and ended up sending out suffocating signals after the initial connection between us was *most definitely* established. What's important here is that the connection was established when he incorrectly assumed I was married. This is why I didn't feel the suffocation vibe immediately; he assumed I was unavailable.

Expectation Kills Attraction

Lance's behavior depicts what is called *expectation*. Expectation is, by far, one of the biggest chemistry killers—in the long, sad history of potent chemistry killers, and second only to putting smelly, dirty hands on her face when trying to initiate intimacy. Lance would have been much better off just taking a deep breath, acting casual about his interest in me, keeping his hungry eyeballs to himself, and allowing me to come his way. Had he done so, I totally would have hung out with him and wanted to get to know him—and probably much more. Nothing about his physical attractiveness had changed—but his energy sure did! It was all about his expectations and desperate need that didn't show up until he found out I wasn't married.

Now, I'm not any more beautiful than any other woman you see on the street. I don't want to come across like, "Look at all these men who want me!" This would be absolutely stupid and useless for me to put in this book. I told you these stories about Frankie and Lance simply because I had the experience of two very handsome men—at two different times in my life, crash and burn any potential of a relationship with me within the first few minutes of us talking—because they didn't realize their inherent value and energetically put their desperate expectations upon me.

My sisters and I have all had hundreds of these kinds of needy and expectant interactions with men. And each of us always has had the exact same knee-jerk reaction: I gotta get away from this guy—like... NOW! Yet, as repulsive as expectation and neediness is, it really is an easy fix.

An Honest Look Within

Sadly, the men who act needy way have NO idea that they are acting this way. Therefore, they have no idea how to turn their dating luck around to their favor. But it's not that hard. Here it is: if you find that woman are dive-bombing out of your way after the first or second date, or before you even make it to the first date, take note of how you usually behave toward them when first meeting them, your level of expectation, and how attached you are to the idea of having a girlfriend. Then... back up. Take a breath, and chill. And allow her to come your way. Then see what happens.

This simple little switch could turn around your whole romantic life. It just might explain the mystery behind your most common relationship frustration: why all the girls you like don't like you back, and all the girls you don't like fall all over themselves trying to get your attention. No—you are not jinxed in love. You simply have your own internal signals crossed.

Stop worrying about your abs, or your hairline, or your cologne. Get your intentions in check. Stop obsessing over the fact that you didn't have the perfect childhood, that your parents didn't love you enough, or the struggles you've had up to this point in your life. All of that is in the PAST for a reason: it does not need to be in the here and now. Forgive what you can, especially yourself, and start developing a true appreciation for YOU.

Get interested in your own life. Right now! Don't wait. It's too important. In fact, put dating on hold for a while, and turn your attention toward yourself. You are an attractive man who can absolutely date attractive, brilliant women. So stop gumming up the process with neediness, fear, and expectation. Become your own best friend. Love yourself. Have your own back. Watch how this affects your life.

Score Point: Be mindful of your internal energy and what your dominant thoughts are when you meet potential dating partners. Because if you shift into, "Oh my gosh! This girl could be the one!" she will feel your energy shift, and very quickly lose interest.

FAIL!! 54 Dating DON'Ts

Boys, admittedly, some of these "don'ts" are very logical. I know that most of you would never commit these cardinal dating sins. But these "don'ts" come straight from the horses' mouths—aka—from women I have interviewed for this book. All of these were big on the list of "don'ts" and were dating deal-breakers for (said) females. So take a gander through this list, and get very real with yourself.

1. Don't send her more than one or two texts, or leave her more than one voicemail if she hasn't responded yet.

2. Don't text her repeatedly throughout the day, even if she keeps texting you back. You need to create some mystery and distance, and texting her constantly shows her you have nothing else going on.

3. In new relationships especially, don't assume she wants you to touch her

4. Don't kiss her when she's not trying to kiss you first. Hint: look her in the eyes in a non-creepy way without moving your face towards her. If she wants a kiss, she will move to kiss you. Or just ask her if you can kiss her. Respect her response.

5. Don't stick your tongue down her throat when you do kiss her for the first time. Actually, keep tongue-play to a minimum during your first few kisses. She will let you know if she wants more.

6. Don't use more than one small spray of cologne

7. Don't wear socks with sandals

8. Don't tell her about your money troubles

9. Don't discuss your depression issues

10. Don't discuss your ex-wife or ex-girlfriend nightmares

11. Don't tell her you are looking for "that one special girl" to complete your life so you can finally be happy! (There's a reason no one has signed up for that yet)

12. Don't go on and on about how much you hate your parents or how much they screwed up your life

13. Don't "split" the bill or make her pay

14. Don't fart and then laugh about it or start up a fart conversation

15. Don't fart and then lock the car windows

16. Don't tell her about the giant triple-flusher you laid that morning

17. Don't talk with food in your mouth (EVER!)

18. Don't have more than one alcoholic drink at dinner—or she'll assume you have a drinking problem

19. Don't be late for your date—and if you are, text or call her right away to let her know

20. Don't suggest you stop by the local titty bar after dinner

21. Don't bitch about the people at your work, your family, or your kids

22. Don't flirt or stare at other attractive women while with her (girls know that guys do this to try to make them jealous—and it always backfires)

23. Don't belch

24. Don't scratch your crotch

25. Don't scratch your armpit and keep eating. Actually. Don't scratch your armpit in front of her.

26. Don't snort and spit

27. Don't spit when you talk—even if you are drooling for her

28. Don't pick your nose in public. (If you must, go to the men's room)

29. Don't blow your nose in front of her or in public (I know Miss Manners touts this as acceptable etiquette, but no one wants to hear it, especially while eating. It's disgusting)

30. Don't try to pick up on her roommate, sister or friend

31. Don't pretend you are the shit or act like a jerk to prove you are confident... because you will come across as an idiot guy whose trying to prove himself

32. Don't brag about your past sexual conquests and girlfriends

33. Don't brag about past drunken or high experiences

34. Don't just talk about yourself

35. Don't lie

36. Don't show up drunk for a date

37. Don't be mean to kids or animals—especially hers!

38. Don't give up your dreams for her

39. Don't spend money you don't have trying to impress her

40. Don't wear the same clothes two days in a row—especially without washing them

41. Don't be jealous

42. Don't drive by her house at night to see if she's home or dating someone else

43. Don't tell her how to dress, how much makeup to wear, or what jewelry to wear

44. Don't manipulate or twist her words

45. Don't talk over her or interrupt her

46. Don't assume you aren't worth her time: you abso-freekin'-lootly are!

47. Don't degrade yourself or cut yourself down

48. Don't invite her over when your house is trashed (clean it up first!)

49. Don't ignore your obligations (work, friends, and family) in order to spend time with her.

50. Don't drunk-text or drunk-dial her

51. Don't touch her face if you have residual of food (or... worse) on your fingers (Blahhh! Yuck...)

52. Beware of stinky feet. If you have genetically sweaty, smelly feet, invest in new shoes every month or so. Don't chance it. Soap up your feet good and proper in the shower... and ALWAYS wear clean socks. Remember: the shoes come off before the pants come down...

53. Don't touch her without permission

54. Don't talk on your phone, check your social media, or text while with her.

Guidelines for Physical Touch

So... you made it to the first date, and things are great. She is responsive and nice, and it seems like she is totally into you. This is the time that you need to keep your wits about you. Don't take liberties (like touching her or kissing her) or invading her personal space bubble in any other way. No excuse to do so is good enough!

Here are a few statements from young women who were turned off by guys invading their personal space too early in the relationship:

- We were eating dinner—our first date together, and I feel his bare foot rubbing up and down my leg. It creeped me out big time!

- We were watching a movie at his place, and he reached over and started playing with my hair—without even asking. I love having my hair played with, but he should have asked me first.

- We were driving around the city with some friends looking at Christmas lights. We were sitting in the back seat. It was really fun at first, but then he put his hand on my knee and wouldn't look at me, and he was trying to be all casual about it. I just wanted to push his hand off my knee and tell him to keep his paws off.

- During the movie, he reached over and grabbed my hand—when it was in my lap—clearly away from him. Then he kept holding it and kissing my fingers. When I tried to pull away, he wouldn't let go. Then he got pissed when I told him to let go and was a jerk the rest of the night.

- It was after the Homecoming dance, and I really, really liked him. We went out to eat and I grabbed his hand and smiled. He got super excited about it and scooted up close to me and started rubbing my arm with his other hand. At first it was fine, but he wouldn't stop rubbing my arm, and it all of the sudden started to annoy me. I wanted him to stop but didn't know how to tell him.

- He smacked my butt while waiting in line at the theater. I was pissed. Never saw him again.

- He kept trying to touch my face and I could smell food on his fingers. It was totally sick. I couldn't get passed it.

- (Hint: After dinner, go to the men's room and wash your hands—with soap—before getting your hands anywhere near her face.)

- We were cuddling on my couch on our second date. I liked him a lot and he seemed super nice. We were watching TV and I fell asleep with my head on his shoulder and his arm around me. When I woke up, he had his hand up my shirt and was groping around! Fucking pervert. It bothered me for a long time. I had a counselor tell me that was a sexual assault because he didn't have my permission.

- We were standing around at a party and he was behind me. He just grabbed me by both hips and pulled me backward and said, "God, I love your ass!" and pushed his crotch onto my butt. I was humiliated and really upset. He had no right to do that. My brother beat him up after he found out.

- He reached over to hold my hand, which was okay. But his hand felt like a dead fish. He didn't really "hold" my hand; he just left it limp.

The last girl here brings up a great point: when you do start to hold hands, don't just let your hand go limp. No girl likes that. Hold her hand gently but firmly, and let go when she wants to.

The Touch DO List:

- DO give her lots of space

- DO let her come to you first

- DO be genuine and open-hearted with your hugs

- DO keep your hands to yourself—until hers are all over you

- DO become acutely aware of her body language and cues

- DO respond appropriately to her body language and cues

- DO let her dictate the amount of touch between you initially

- Do take the "recessive" position, and let her come to you

The Touching DON'T List:

- Don't grope her

- Don't cling to her

- Don't drool on her

- Don't get in her "bubble" before she feels safe with you

- Don't take the liberty of touching any part of her body with any part of your body

- Don't manhandle her

- Don't smack her butt

- Don't touch her and "look away" as if you don't know what you are doing

- Don't get annoyed if she pulls away when you try to touch her. She's just not ready yet. This isn't personal.

Remember guys: she needs to feel safe with you before she will let her guard down and let you in. Guys tend to push the envelope because they think they are helping the intimacy in the relationship move along. But it has the opposite effect, because her subconscious guard will go up—and she won't trust you. It's far better to leave her wanting more after a date than let her feel even a little bit invaded.

Back to Johnny

The biggest reason Johnny… er… John had such amazing luck with meeting and dating new women was the fact that he knew to hang back and let them come to him. His "out of her bubble" demeanor, coupled with his wide-open heart and a vested interest in his own life, drew women in by sheer intrigue.

Of course, we, as his sisters, didn't really "get" what all the fuss was about; this was Johnny. He was just our annoying little brother who slept too much, ate too much, never helped with chores, left his dirty socks and underwear laying around, never made his bed, and brought all his annoying little friends over to the house to eat all of our food and dirty our pool with their sweaty sports-playing bodies. In hindsight, of course, I do get what all the fuss was about; Johnny was a girl magnet because of his genuine, fun-loving, and laid-back self.

He never felt desperate around girls—since he was happy with who he was. This made him show up in a very different energy than most other guys—who are usually desperate for sex and feel like they need a girlfriend in order to be happy. Girls naturally felt safe around John, and were drawn into his bubble... and that's where he worked his magic.

Note that Johnny was never EVER rude or indifferent towards women. He never pretended that he didn't care about them. He was never domineering or insulting. He didn't shut down or come across "stone faced." He would never manipulate, invalidate, verbally abuse, or manhandle. Ever. He was so genuine, kind, fun-loving, and confident that women would melt into a gooey puddle of desire anytime he walked into a room.

The Dos and Don'ts of Kissing

Kissing is another subject that definitely deserves some attention... because a lot of guys simply do it wrong—and have no idea! The very first point to consider: your breath. Remember Johnny's first note to self? *Brush teeth. Floss. Use mouthwash. Always...* Obviously, most of you will do this anyway before your date. But what about after dinner? You don't want to kiss her with pieces of food stuck in your teeth or the smell of scampi on your breath. Especially, if you go out to dinner and eat onions, garlic, or spices, that's gonna show up in your breath, even hours later. After dinner go to the men's room and, while your washing the smell of food off your hands (see the DOs of touch in last section) at least rinse out your mouth. So.... you have clean hands and a clean mouth: two LESS barriers to deal with—affectionately speaking!

The movie *Hitch* with Will Smith contains some great relationship advice for men. One of the best pieces of advice he gives about the first kiss is this:

"This is what most guys do. They rush in to take the kiss. But you're not most guys. See, the secret to a kiss is to go 90% of the way... and then hold. (For how long?) As long as it takes... for her to come the other 10%." (Hitch, Sony Pictures, 2005)

In other words, you can move your face toward her—90% of the way—"and then hold." Let her come to you the other 10% of the way. Though here is my input: if she turns her head or otherwise avoids your coming in close, simply back up. Don't take it personally! Just give her space. She is still learning about you and may not be ready for a kiss just yet.

Remember, one of the New Relationship Turn Offs from earlier in the book: *forceful kisses involving the sticking your tongue down her throat and into her pancreas.* Be very cautious with tongue-heavy kisses with a new girl. Start soft and sweet... she will let you know if she wants more. If she is still unsure of you, forceful, tongue-heavy kisses could creep her out—and up goes her guard.

On the other hand, you don't want to be too small-mouthed or "tight lipped" about it either. There is nothing worse than kissing a guy with super tight, nervous lips! It feels like… kissing a turtle. So relax the mouth. Relax the jaw. Relax the tongue. Go 90% of the way and hold. When she moves in the other 10%, kiss her sweetly and softly. Keep your tongue in your mouth. Don't over-pucker. Just... relax and kiss her for a few seconds, then back up a little, and see if she comes in for another kiss. If she doesn't, don't take the liberty of kissing her again. Don't cop an attitude. Don't get pissed. Just gently let her go and give her more time to decide—with no pressure.

Let's look at a few real-life examples of kissing turn offs from women:

- He walked me to my car and just grabbed me and started kissing me—like he was totally horny. I was like what the hell is wrong with you? It was our first date! I was so not into him like that.

- He was one of those hippie tree-huggers. He stunk. His armpits stunk. His breath stunk. Even his hair stunk. He couldn't figure out why I wouldn't kiss him goodnight, and why I never saw him again.

- He was like a totally sloppy kisser and got spit all over me. He opened his mouth way too wide and drooled all over my face. It was totally sick.

- His breath smelled like vomit and wine. There was no way in hell I was going to kiss that freak.

- When he kissed me, he kept making really crazy moaning noises, like you would make during sex. It was weird for a first kiss, especially since I wasn't that into him.

- He had super chapped lips and when he kissed me, it felt like sandpaper. I just kept wondering if he was sick or something.

Yeah, chapped lips are a huge turnoff and are the result of dehydration. Your body is more than 75 percent water, and dehydration can cause more problems for you than chapped lips—including sexual and emotional problems. (When you are dehydrated, your circulatory and nervous system both have a harder time working. Sexually speaking, your penis needs blood flow. If you are dehydrated, your blood is thick and viscous, and your circulation can become impaired. Further, dehydrated semen is super thick and gooey and your body will have a harder time producing it. Plus—thick goo isn't super appealing to most girls—if she happens to see it, feel it, or taste it.

Emotionally speaking, a dehydrated body will be very depressed. With dehydration, nerve and blood flow are both impaired. Dehydration leads to toxicity build up in the body and can lead to a sickly appearance and low energy. I bet you had no idea that drinking water had ANYTHING to do with your sex life!

The Kissing DON'T List

- DON'T assume she wants you to kiss her

- DON'T kiss her with rank breath

- DON'T force kisses on her

- DON'T stick your tongue down her throat—until she shows you that that's what she wants

- DON'T cop an attitude if she acts timid or pulls away

- DON'T drool all over her mouth or face. That's a potential "gross-out" factor. Swallow first and often!

- DON'T moan or make outrageously passionate noises—not for the first kiss.

- DON'T be a kissing bully. Let her come to you.

The Kissing DO List

- DO brush your teeth. Floss. Use mouthwash. Always.

- DO rinse your mouth out after dinner

- DO follow Hitch's 90/10 rule; go in 90% of the way, and let her come the other 10%

- DO kiss her gently the first few times. She will let you know if she wants more

- DO relax your lips, jaw, tongue, and face before kissing

- DO respect her boundaries—and keep a good attitude even if she pulls away

- DO stay hydrated; it prevents chapped lips and keeps your body healthy

The Secret to Rocking Her World in Bed

There are about a thousand sex "how to" books on the market today. Most of them focus on the "mechanics" of sex (e.g.: insert slot A into slot B and pump at a rate of 2.6 thrusts per second and from a 90% angle and with velocity of 7 and force of 9.9; if bedroom fan is on consider wind resistance=.089 and increase thrust force by .012...).

These books don't give any insight into what is TRULY needed for a man to seduce a woman and get her to fall in love with him: your heart. Your willingness to be you. Sorry if that sounds sappy, but that's just the way it is, boys. The confusing part of all this is that you need to do this from a place of confidence—not desperation or neediness—neither of which have ANYTHING to do with the heart.

The #1 most important thing to remember is that you need to approach her with your heart... not your head... either one. A guy could read every "how to give her a screaming orgasm using ordinary household objects" book on the market, but if he approaches sex with a logical mind, the energy exchange that is the heart-and-soul of insanely good sex will be missing, and then all you are left with physical gratification on both sides... and you will not be a memorable lover.

Heart energy flow is really important for great chemistry. Only a true love connection can give girls what she really craves: passionate intimacy. Women crave intimate connection with men. They can't get this through a toy... nor can you deliver this with a mass of *how to* knowledge.

A lot of guys look to sexual skill building as a way to help boost their bedroom confidence. But you're not most guys. You now know that, without an engaged heart, sex falls flat. Therefore, if you can pair your heart energy and vulnerability with your "how to give a girl a great orgasm" knowledge, then you will probably bed her famously. But know that your *how to give her an orgasm* skills are just the icing on the cake. Not even the icing on the cake—it's the decorations on top of the icing on the cake. The most important thing is this: you must be willing to be vulnerable with her—without being needy. That is a skill that is finely tuned and you will master as you get more confident overall.

Your Subconscious Fears: Identified

Many men have subconscious fears about sex and relationships. Shutting down your heart is a reaction to these subconscious fears. In all honesty, some of these fears are warranted; there are a lot of clingy, needy, manipulative women out there that make the dating and romantic world a scary, confusing, and thorny place to dwell.

But there are a lot of awesome, wonderful girls out there, too. And early in the relationship, it's not always easy to tell which girls are which. Therefore, it is far better to make informed decisions about your dating life than it is to make decisions out of subconscious fear, raging hormones, and a desperate search for a willing-and-ready sperm receptacle. Let's look at some of the most common relationship fears that come up for men that keep them from having outrageously awesome sexual experiences:

- Fear of making mistakes or looking like an idiot in bed

- Fear of getting hurt (sometimes its easier to just check out)

- Fear of not satisfying her in bed

- Fear she won't like your body (or penis)

- Fear of being "stuck" with a clingy woman after having sex

- Fear of a woman's relationship expectations after having sex

- Fear of letting go of a relationship —even though you're no longer into her—because its familiar and "safe"

- Fear of lonliness

- Fear of just not being good enough for her

Wait a Minute... How Can I Be Vulnerable and Confident at the Same Time??

There is no contradiction here. Vulnerability and confidence can easily exist within one human. It is important for you to comprehend exactly what it means to be *vulnerable and confident at the same time.* Men who don't understand this will never be able to truly become a memorable lover who rocks her world and leaves her cooing like a baby dove. It's a short story that one of my clients wrote me for this book.

Gail and Scott

Gail writes: I have an ex-boyfriend named Scott who was one of my most memorable, incredibly awesome relationships EVER. When I met Scott, I was dating three other guys, and liked all of them. I wasn't sleeping with any of them; I was still trying to decide which guy I liked enough to start dating exclusively.

Initially, Scott was kind of on the back burner. But I did feel chemistry with him, and decided to give him a chance. We went on a few dates, and had some great times. He was confident and fun—and turned out to be a really cool guy. I liked him. A lot.

Scott came over to my place one night after work. I had just gotten out of the shower; no makeup, hair still wet. I was in a plain tee shirt and pajama shorts—so not feeling not super sexy. He sat down on the couch and I sat across his lap and he hugged me. I had been hard-core craving him for days, and falling into his arms felt amazing. But he seemed to be somewhere else in his mind; he just kind of half-heartedly rubbed my back, wouldn't look at me, and couldn't carry on a decent conversation. I got a little annoyed I was craving passion and connection. *(Remember—this is what is the most important to women)*. But he obviously wasn't interested—or so it seemed. He kept looking off in other directions, staring at my very boring apartment walls, pictures, looking at my plants, my television (which wasn't even on), etc... What I concluded was, *Oh well... he's just not that into me.* I pulled away from him with the intention to stand up and said calmly, "You know, maybe this was a mistake, Scott. You seem to be really distracted tonight and not that into me."

He looked at me and caught his breath, his eyes wide, looking scared and shocked. "Are you kidding? I can't even look at you. You're so beautiful. You intimidate the hell out of me. I'm sorry. I'm just scared. Please... please... don't get up. Stay ... right here..." He pulled me to his chest and hugged me close. I felt his guard drop and his heart burst open. "Gail. I just don't know how to be here with you and feeling what I'm feeling."

Was it a game? A ploy to get me in bed? I don't think so. That kind of energy is something I can detect pretty well. In this moment, he felt extremely genuine and so loving. In that moment that there was no question where his heart was—with me. Wow. Melt my heart... I was suddenly putty in his arms.

Review of Gail and Scott:

Gail was caught completely off guard... and totally taken. Not just with what Scott said, but with him owning up to his fears and his willingness to be so vulnerable with her in this crucial moment. Only a confident man can do this. There is something sexy—and very attractive—about just owning it... without being needy, clingy, or desperate. Scott was very confident in who he was and didn't need Gail to "complete" him. But even a confident man gets intimidated by the woman he loves (or really likes). The difference is that truly confident men are able to take that leap into their heart and be vulnerable. Whereas insecure men just act from their brain and never plunk into their hearts to allow the energy to finally flow.

Had Scott been less confident, he might have stood up and said, "Whatever, Gail! Fine. I'll leave then!" and off he would go—with his pride... and blue balls... and Gail on the other side of the door, determined to never see him again. Scott's confidence and willingness to own his feelings made their sex off-the-charts awesome. They were together for almost five years and, according to Gail, their sex life was always amazing.

Does Size Really Matter?

First, almost every guy on the planet worries whether or not his pecker is big enough. And this is almost always an irrational fear. The "maybe my penis is too small" fear stems from a subconscious lack of confidence overall.

Guess what? (Since I changed his name in this book I can tell you this) Gail confessed that Scott's penis wasn't really all that big... and she was secretly very, very happy about it. "It didn't hurt, and there was no pretention, nothing for him to prove. You see all the bullshit about size and all that crap. That's like saying a guy can only like a girl if she's got big boobs. That's total bullshit. Scott and I just connected on an insanely pure level—which feels way better than any Pringles-can-size penis attached to a less-confident or asshole of a man... and I've been with both! No thank you!" (Gail was kind of a feisty... and kind of bitchy at times. But she was really intelligent, very pretty, and she knew what she wanted – a guy with a heart that was bigger than his member.) During one of our last sessions, Gail said this to me. "Aaliya, you need to write this in your book. Cuz guys need to pull their heads out of their asses and stop worrying so much about their dick size. You know, most of the time, guys with big, huge dicks are just total idiots. They think they don't need to try or something. But any quality girl can see right through it, and these guys end up with the bleach blonde bimbos with huge collagen lips, total plastic and no soul. Which usually turns out to be the perfect girl for him. Ew. No thanks! Give me a guy with a medium sized dick, a good heart, a sharp mind and a sense of morality- and I'll show you the guy I want to marry."

Well now. I don't think I could have said any of this any better, myself! Thank you, Gail!

Heart-based sexual connection fuels the passionate intimacy needed for you to rock her world. THIS is the reason for the "size doesn't matter" advice that so many men obsess over, and very few ever understand. The only time that size does matter is with women who are after mindless sex for physical gratification. And that's a sad, lonely woman right there—with her own versions of fear and what is really important. But when it comes to chemistry, intimacy, and love, any humbly-confident man can powerfully deliver to the woman he really loves—no matter what size his penis is. How do I mean? Well, if you are a confident guy, and you are able to approach relationships with an honest, open heart, and a girl is really into you, then she will love your penis, no matter what size it is. And, you will not worry if it's too small. If it feels good and it works, you both will be thrilled with your ability to connect sexually. Make sense? Good... now read on, and we will discuss why logical lovers are the worst kind of lovers on the planet.

"But... But... But... I Still Want a Bigger Penis!"

Okay. I hear you, Buddy. With all this being said about heart based vulnerability, confidence, and connection, most guys still want to know if it's possible to increase the size of their penis. Short answer: yes. And I don't think this book would be complete if I didn't point you in the right direction here. ***Please note: I'm not a doctor and can't give you medical advice. You take responsibility in whatever you choose to do or not do in response to the research you do on these websites.***

After extensive research and wading through a lot of bullshit, I've discovered that there ARE some really simple yet potent exercises that can increase a man's penis length and girth, as well as his sexual desire and performance. I'm not going to discuss the details of these exercises in this book, but I have listed the website links and points of reference for you here:

***www.pelongi.com/en/** German website translated to English: Videos and instruction: 53 exercises for increasing penis length and girth- including penis weights- which seem extremely intense, but promising. But USE CAUTION! I know a few men who have caused severe damage to their male parts from sex-gone wrong, manhandling themselves too roughly, and other penile-damaging activities. The recover was painful, long, and, at times, expensive.*

***topmens.info/en/** Information for improving male sexual perform- ance, penis size, correcting erectile dysfunction and premature ejaculation*

***Look up VigRX Oil:** I'm not an affiliate here, and don't get any kickback. I just found it in my research and I like that it is all natural, about $50, and simple to use.*

***Note:** an interesting observation I made during my research: like many big-pharma influenced industries, the available American-based information on this subject paints a bleak picture for men looking to improve their penis size and overall sexual performance. (Don't believe it!) Sadly, in America, taking your sexual health into your own hands goes against the prescribed narrative of using expensive medications or surgery. So research these practices. Use them judiciously- and at your own risk!*

***Supplements:** There are also many vitamins, herbs and supplements available for men's sexual health. (Many denounced / downplayed by the American Big Pharma influence). Maca, Zinc and Ginseng are but a few of the powerful supplements available. One word of caution: read the labels. Be wary of any products containing soy. Soy is estrogenic (estrogen is a strong female hormone) which can be extremely counterproductive to your efforts to improve your sexual health and appearance. (Moobs, smaller penis, lack of male drive can all result from an influence of estrogen.)*

Logical Lovers SUCK!

Many of the women I interviewed for this book talked about short-lived relationships with guys—some of whom were hung like Trojan horses—but who approached the whole sex-and-intimacy thing with their egos and dedication to *showin' her how it's done!* These men put their entire focus onto their performance and physical qualities, and never shifted into their heart space the way Scott was able to do with Gail. With the "logical lovers," the energy just never flows. In some cases, sex is even disgusting, because, for the logical lover, it is reduced to a merely physical act, with no energy flow. And those romps end with something like, *Get off me. We're done. Sorry, Buddy, You'll have to take care of that beast yourself...*

It's normal to get intimidated and scared when in bed with a girl. Scott with Gail was no exception. The difference was his ability to be honest with her and own his fear—which broke down his walls and allowed them to connect on an authentic level. Because of his ability to stay in his heart with her, they consistently had incredible sex throughout their five years together. His willingness to be vulnerable was wayyy more important that any amount of skill he brought to the bedroom. It's nice to bring skills; that's for sure. But if a man isn't willing to be vulnerable? Then his sexual skills will mean squat. The heart: it makes all other pieces fall into place.

Blue-Ball Blind

Here's a question I get a lot from men: *I'm so horny! There's this girl and I really don't like her but she is all over me. Can I just bang her?*

Short answer: I don't recommend it. Remember the notion of being your own best friend? Having your own back? Yeah, it matters here. Pre-sex clingy girls tend to turn into post-sex nightmares for guys, and you invite a whole slew of problems into your life by just sexing the desperately willing and available chick... and worrying about consequences later.

Psycho? Break-ups? Suicidal threats? Pregnancy? Whining? Bitching? Moaning? If you aren't all that into an already clingy girl, having sex with her is a surefire way to get her to invade your life and become a Stage Five Clinger. In the next section, *Into the Jungle—Where Brave Men Fear to Tread* we will do some exploring of these consequences. Not the most fun thing to read—but definitely helpful and it could save you a lifetime of headaches and grief!

You are MUCH better off taking your horniness out on Rosy Palm... rather than an already clingy chick who is available-and-willing. Heck, Buddy! You can deflate a blow up doll and stuff it into your closet. Blow up dolls don't go psycho, they don't show up at your work unannounced, they don't get pregnant, and they don't call or text you 100 times a day, whining and crying, calling you nasty names, and trying to get you to love them.

Okay, the blow up doll thing is kinda... no... really creepy. But my point is that... yes. You will get horny. And yes, there are probably a few girls around who would hump you in a heartbeat. Again, the problem is that you invite a whole slew of problems into your life when you have sex with a needy, available girl.

Hold out for the chick you really like... the one you really connect with, the one you really crave. You know the difference. ;)

Into the Jungle—Where Brave Men Fear to Tread...

Fair warning... the next few sections get a little ugly. It's going to take us into the deeper part of the romantic jungle, where all men fear to tread... or even think about treading. But this exploration is necessary, because the best prevention of any problem is knowledge, and I wouldn't be doing my job if I didn't acquaint you with the taming of these ferocious jungle beasts so you can stay them off in the future.

The next section we are going to be discussing some really serious, sticky, awful topics. You know... things like the best way to dump an emotionally needy girlfriend, how to handle her inevitable freak-outs, what to do if she threatens suicide, the perils of dating a complete psycho, unplanned pregnancy (is the baby really yours?) and how to walk through these awful jungle tangles when you've got the rest of your life in front of you. My apologies if things get heavy, but it will only be temporarily, while I spell out the nitty-gritty details of each of these difficult predicaments that many men will face at some time in their lives. In this way, you will be amply prepared if and when the ever do show up for you.

Okay... give me your hand. I will walk through this jungle with you. And don't worry, I will be with you the whole time... ☺

Jungle Beast #1: The Stage-Five Clinger (SFC)

In the movie Wedding Crashers, Jeremy Gray (Vince Vaughn) tries to escape the emotional claws of his brand new love interest, Gloria Cleary (Isla Fisher). He tells his partner in crime, John Beckwith (Owen Wilson), "I gotta get out of here—pronto! I've got a Stage Five Clinger!" And every guy in the audience busted out laughing, because they knew exactly what that meant.

If you're a good guy, chances are you have had (or are currently in the thick of) the God-awful experience of trying to dump a Stage Five Clinger (SFC). SFC is a girl who digs her emotional claws into a guy and will not let go! She is the girl who shows up at your house unannounced, shows up at your work with a plate of cookies, wearing too much makeup and a racy yellow spandex dress that would put Wolverine to shame. An SFC is notorious for gushing that terrible, needy energy that sucks the life right out of you. Chances are you struggle with the prospect of dumping her... because you know she will freak out and cry, and make you feel like the meanest bastard on the face of the planet. "You owe her!!" after all... or at least, that's her take on it.

Guess what, Dude? You don't owe her anything!!! <insert happy-dance here> You just need to muster up the courage to be honest with her. And if you can't quite wrap your brain around that, try this advice on for size: dating a woman out of guilt is not fair to her either. You will eventually hurt her much more than if you are honest with her in the first place, and you will keep her from finding a guy who could truly appreciate her. If you decide it is too much trouble and upset to break up with her, and you end up staying with her anyway, be prepared, for you will eventually be living a life of pure hell. Trust me. Cut the ties. I'm going to discuss how to do that effectively in a moment.

Please, for the sake of everyone involved, do not date (or marry!) a woman out of guilt or obligation! It is psychologically devastating with profound, life-long effects.

If you have ever had to dump a past lover, girlfriend, spouse, or just some gal that was infatuated with you and wouldn't leave you alone, you may still be feeling pretty guilty about it. And if you are STILL dating her... kinda sorta... because you don't want to hurt her feelings, at least take a step back and review the situation logically: you cringe every time she calls or texts you, and you feel "doomed" to live out a life with her until she simply gets sick of your shit. (She won't). That's not love, nor any semblance of it. And what she feels for you isn't love—it's called "infatuation." And it feels shitty... huh? That's because you are essentially supporting a very defunct pattern in her. That isn't virtuous. That's called living a lie. And there is nothing virtuous about just trying to be nice so she doesn't get her heart broken.

You can't just put this on the back burner. Instead of playing this miserable waiting game, take action. (I'm about to tell you what action to take—don't worry.) And whatever you do, don't pretend you still love her; that can really hack up your life and keep you from meeting another really awesome girl who truly would rock your world!

Why Good Guys Get Labeled as Pigs

Most men don't know how to dump a girl, so they try to adjust their life in a way that they can still-kinda-sorta carry on with her and avoid that inevitable firestorm of a breakup. These goodhearted men simultaneously try the slowly-backing away from her route, in hopes she takes the hint... which she doesn't. In fact, she slowly backing up approach increases her desperation and, click-by-click, turns up her SFC dial. At that point, even the nicest guy can turn into an insufferable prick—showing her blatant signs of disrespect, insolence, and manipulation. This is his last-ditch attempt to get her to break up with him... and, of course, that doesn't work either.

Then hell really breaks loose; she starts pushing back with all sorts of snotty, manipulative demands and pressing for a commitment. He is completely overwhelmed and inundated, starts avoiding her calls, gives ambiguous answers about his weekend plans, and, in order to get his sexual and intimacy needs met, starts dating other girls behind her back. The SFC will eventually find out about his new girls (by stalking, putting up hidden cameras or recording devices, hiring a private detective, hacking email/social media accounts, or, in more than one case that I've worked with, will break into his home and hide in the closet, trying to "catch him in the act." Can you say, "psycho," boys and girls?

And all the while, this poor guy is just trying to figure out a way to get rid of this chick who has made his life a living, breathing nightmare. He is engaged in a sort of "split living" as I call it—meaning he is trying to smooth the waters with SFC and pursue new romantic territory at the same time. This is exactly why men get dubbed as "pigs."

But most men are NOT pigs; they are just really lousy at dumping (and being honest with) desperate women. By the way, you can breathe a sigh of relief; the girl who extreme-stalks you is definitely not someone you want in your future anyway, and you have my permission to dump her. You can be respectful, yes, but you need to be a RSD: a Respectfully Stern Dumper.

First off, unless she is truly dangerous, it is both disrespectful and cowardly to break up with someone through a text message. Meeting her face-to-face is preferred—and the most gentleman-like thing to do. If face-to-face is not an option, at least call her up on the phone. Just... don't leave a breakup message on her voicemail. (That's even worse than a text message!) Actually, if at all possible, have this conversation at (or in front of) her house, so she doesn't need to drive home while upset.

If You Live Together

If you two live together and you want to break up, there are other factors involved, such as who will be moving out? How will you split up your furniture, dishes, bank accounts, and beds? Who will get your pets? Or, you two may have kids together. I cannot comment on the process of legally splitting up your stuff, custody, visitation, mitigation, etc... because that simply isn't my place. However, I most certainly can comment on the importance of attitude: be as kind and as fair as possible—even if she gets nasty with you. She may want to try and "hoard" all of your stuff, but know this is simply because she is emotionally reeling, and her hoarding your stuff that you have together is her subconscious way of trying to "hang on" to the relationship. Have some empathy for her, though do not cheat yourself out what is fair either. If she gets angry and nasty, its simply because she is emotionally hurting. While it is not up to you to "fix" her feelings, it is up to you to be as kind as possible. At the very least, be civil.

I've known many women who, in the midst of a breakup, take their boyfriends' credit card and go on a shopping spree or two. If you think she would be one of those to do that (or even if you don't) you may want to put your wallet under lock and key. A heartbroken woman with no self-esteem can cause untold damage in the lives of men. Be careful. And think ahead.

Crystal Clear Intention

When you do talk to her—either face-to-face or over the phone, you need to be very clear with her about the intention of the talk. No fumbling with your words, no double-talk or back tracking. Just the simple, very clear truth. If she is a woman who is normally violent, emotionally reactive and has shown signs of dangerousness during past arguments, then I definitely recommend breaking up via phone call. In some cases, an email may be appropriate too; just make sure it is very clear, as kind as possible, and doesn't blame or shame her—or yourself.

Let's quickly look at The Wrong Way and The Right Way to break up with the SFC:

The Wrong Way

Yeah... hey Darla. Thanks for all the shit you've done for me. But I like, met another girl that has these awesome big boobs and a way better body than you and I can't wait to bang her. So get lost, bitch.

The Right Way

Darla, I really appreciate everything you've done for me. And even though it's going to be hard on both of us, it's time for us to go our separate ways. I know you will make another guy very happy. I don't want to keep you from discovering that since I can't show up for you the way you deserve a guy to show up for you. (That's it, dude! Now shut up! Don't plan to stick around any longer than a couple of minutes.)

She may start yelling or crying, and will ask something like, "What do you mean? We can still be friends and hang out... right?"

Your response should be something like, "I'm sorry, no, definitely not. That's not going to help anything. This needs to be over, so we can both move on with our lives."

When she starts yelling louder or crying harder, she will say something like, "How dare you do this to me, after all I've done for you?! It's easy for you to move on, but how am I supposed to move on? I gave up everything for you! And now you are dumping me like yesterday's trash! Fuck you, you stupid bastard! Fuck you!" (First, let her rant. When she finally pauses long enough for you to get a word in, your response should be something like:

"I know this is rough. But this just needs to be done. I've felt very suffocated lately, like you can't be happy without me, and I just can't live that way. I'm sorry you gave up everything for me. I never asked you to do that. In any case, I am sticking with this decision. There is no changing my mind. We are definitely broken up as of now."

I am not one to advocate dishonesty. But I'm going to make one small exception here, especially if Darla is off the charts upset and has shown any sign of violence, or has cast any threat of violence—

toward you, herself, or anyone you might start to date. Here it is: if she asks you if you met someone else, or are dating another girl, TELL HER NO. (Even if you are). She is in such an unreasonable, anxious state, that she won't be able to process the thought that you are involved with someone else. This could cause things to escalate really quickly. That, and there is no reason to torture her with thoughts of you being with another woman. Just say, "No, that's not it at all." Don't get sucked into a conversation of trying to prove yourself. You are done here. If you feel compelled to give her a hug, do so. But don't linger. Keep it brief.

At this point, it is time for you to leave. This is about the extent of the conversation of a breakup talk. What is extremely important is that you are very clear and avoid vague or ambiguous talk. A woman needs to know exactly where she stands—with a very hard line drawn in **cement.** This way, she won't overanalyze later if you were really breaking up with her? Or if you were just wanting a little "down time" or if you were not really breaking up with her but were just angry with her? (Etc... etc... etc...) Grieving women often overanalyze breakups; it's part of how they work through their emotions. Just know that there is nothing else you can say that will make this process easier on her... and you need to let her walk through her own heartbreak instead of trying to "cushion her fall" by sorta kinda trying to stay with her while she gets her emotional stability back—because with you in the picture, she never will.

If you are NOT clear with her on exactly where you stand (meaning, "we are definitely over—no questions about it!") she will be in constant pining away after you mode, and when the other shoe does finally drop, you will be labeled a "pig" for "leading her on." Because what it will look like to her and the rest of the world is **not** that you're a good guy who just feels guilty about hurting her, but that you can't make up your mind, and are "just using her" while you figure it out. Tell me I'm not right?!

The DON'Ts of Breaking Up

1) DON'T have the break-up talk in front of **her** friends, family, coworkers, etc...

2) DON'T have the breakup talk in front of any of **your** friends, family, coworkers, etc...

Reasoning: This is a very private conversation and you do not want to embarrass her. She's got enough to deal with over then next couple of weeks (or months) in trying to put her heart and life back together.

3) DON'T break up with her after you've been drinking or using drugs. You need to both be SOBER.

4) DON'T break up with her right before Valentine's Day, her birthday, right before an important event (like her debut presentation

at her work or the night before a final exam), or the day after her dog died. That's just cruel.

5) DON'T ask her for "one final blow-job" as she's walking out the door.

6) DON'T dump her for her sister or friend. Be a man. MOVE ON.

7) DON'T act ambiguous about your decision after your breakup talk. What's done is done is done. This relationship is done. (E.g.: Don't agree to meet up with her to *just talk.)*

8) Don't bang her during a dry spell.

9) Don't take her phone calls or otherwise listen to her rant about how much she loves you, needs you and is desperate to "work this out."

10) DON'T fall into the guilt trap that you "ruined her life."

Some women REALLY pour on the guilt and are very good at roping men back into their dysfunction. Stand strong. Don't answer her calls. If she texts or emails you over the next few days or weeks (which she will) you can just ignore most of them.

Typically, after-breakup voicemails, emails, and texts from upset women are always either guilt-laying—whereby she blames you for ruining her life, or they are insulting and hurtful. In the case of the latter, she might say / text some really mean things, your physical body, the size of your pecker, or whatever else she can do to emotionally trigger you and try and engage you in an argument—

because some attention from you is better than no attention from you. Ignore these statements as much as possible. At most, look at them as ample reassurance that you did the right thing by breaking up with her. If you do respond at all, make it a short and considerate reply, reiterating that the relationship is over:

Darla, I'm sorry that this breakup has been so hard on you. But your texts aren't helping anything. My decision is final. We both need to move on. I truly hope the best for you.

Or:

Darla, I know you are upset. And I'm sorry for that. But please stop texting me these hurtful messages. My decision is final. We both need to move on.

I recommend that you save your texts/ emails/ messages—for many reasons. First, you can simply "forward" them back to her when she starts in again—and let her see the "FWD:" on those messages, and, you can forward them to her family and friends who are blaming you for "not letting Darla know where she stands with you." (Not that you need to prove anything to anyone, but being able to substantiate your actions will minimize their ability to manipulate you and vie for your time... and sanity. Then.. no pig label cometh.

After a breakup, do not feel obligated to continue a friendship with her in order to pacify her. Yeah, it's important to treat her with respect. But it is also important to treat her authentically. Her broken heart is not for you to fix. Her broken heart is her to fix. And you breaking up with her because you are not attracted to her anymore doesn't make you a jerk. It doesn't make you a pig. It just makes you real, and a man who can act from a place of truth and integrity. She—not you—needs to figure out how to get unstuck from her own SFC mode. You don't need to figure it out for her. Your presence in her life will delay her progress—not help it.

Jungle Beast #2: She Keeps Showing Up

You can ignore her knocking and pleading, and ask your room-mates to do the same. At most, send her a text: *Darla, we are done. I'm not going to come out to talk to you. Whatever you need to say to me can be done through a text or email.* If she persists, threatens you, destroys any property, or breaks into your house, call the police.

What if she keeps showing up at your work? This is a difficult situation because we usually need to keep our demeanor professional in our work environments. No matter, if you work in an office, let the receptionist know that you can't talk to her or that you are unavailable. If you work somewhere that you can't avoid her, keep your conversation very brief, reiterating that you are broken up: *Darla, please remember that we broke up a week ago? I can't talk to you.* If necessary, let your supervisor know your situation so that he understands that you are not asking your ex to come into your work to visit. If you work in a restaurant and she sits in your section (creepy—but some women do!) respectfully request that another server takes the table, or respectfully ask her to leave and do not engage with her again. If she is raising a scene, you can solicit the help of your manager to ask her to leave. Remember, if she threatens you or destroys property, call the police.

Jungle Beast #3: She Threatens to Kill Herself

So what do you do with an ex who tells you that, if she can't be with you, then she "just wants to die?" That she "just can't take the pain of not being with you!"? This is called *suicidal ideation* and can really be a big, scary beast in the relationship jungle to the nice guy.

Suicidal ideation can show up subtly—as a passive comment of "there's nothing really to live for" or "I wish I would have just died in that car accident last year…" to blatant threats of "I've got the pills in my hand and am ready to swallow them!" Here's the thing: it is not (repeat… NOT) up to you to determine if she really is suicidal or not. Leave that to the professionals—which we will get to in a moment.

Sadly, broken-hearted and needy women use this as a last ditch effort to get a man's attention, and it really can be extremely upsetting and confusing for guys. But not you! You handle it with great skill and in the best interest of all involved. Because I am going to tell you exactly how to do it.

The good news here is, she is finally getting the hint that it truly is over between you two, and, once you properly handle this situation, she should leave you alone for good. But you need to handle it in a way that not only helps to keep her safe, but minimizes her ability to manipulate you. I want you to handle the SFC's suicide threat exactly like this. Do not deviate:

1) Call her or text her and ask her where she is. Ask her for the exact address if you don't know it. Write it down.

2) Text her or tell her in a very sincere tone, "Gosh, Darla, I had no idea you were this upset. Don't worry. Just hang tight. I'm calling the crisis team in for you." Then hang up and CALL the crisis team. Don't just say you are going to do it. DO it! The National Suicide Prevention Line is 1-800-784-2433. You can also do a quick internet search in your own state for "crisis prevention" or "suicide hotline" with your zip code.

What to Expect on the Crisis Call

The crisis teams will ask you a series of questions: what your ex girlfriend said to you that makes you concerned that she may be suicidal, whether or not she has the means (e.g.: gun, pills, razors), if she has had any prior suicide attempts, substance abuse, mental illness diagnosis, etc... This is not the time to downplay or second-guess yourself or your concerns; tell them exactly what she said (or texted you) and answer all questions as honestly as possible, to the best of your ability. But don't be afraid to say, "I don't know" to any questions if you don't know the answer. Do not minimize anything, and don't exaggerate either. Make sure the crisis operator knows that you recently broke up with her and she isn't taking it very well, and that she has threatened to kill herself. It is also perfectly appropriate in this situation to call her family members and/or responsible friends and give them a heads-up. This is what you tell them: Darla called me really upset a little while ago and is making threats against her own life. I called the crisis team already and they are on their way. She is at _____ (place). Don't engage them much past this, especially if they start blaming you for "bringing her to this point." That's an argument you just don't need to have. Ever. You can just say, "I'm sorry you feel that way. I do need to get going now. Goodbye." Then hang up!

If the crisis team stated that they will not be going out to check on her or call her, let the family member(s)/ friend(s) know. Tell them, "The crisis operator doesn't think Darla's threats are serious enough to follow up on it. But I'm still really concerned and wanted to let you know about it and let you know that somebody should probably check up on her tonight. Obviously, that can't be me. Please message me back when you get this." If you don't get a response from any of her family members, call them again. Be persistent. If her relative or friend texts you back something accusatory or rude, such as, "And why can't it be you staying with her tonight, playa?" Just ignore it. You're done here.

YES—Darla will be madder than a one-legged waitress working at I-hop. She will call you every name in the book for "telling her family her personal business" and will curse you out like a sailor with a bad case of hemorrhoids. To which you calmly reply, "You threatened to kill yourself. What did you think I was gonna do?" And then... CONVERSATION OVER! Long about now, you should delete her and block her from your social media sites. And if you can't block her calls/texts, consider getting a new phone number.

This approach has numerous benefits. First, if she is just bluffing with her suicide threat—which is most often the case, she will let you know it very quickly. She will say, "Oh, I'm alright. You don't need to call the crisis team!" Or "I'm just trying to express to you how upset I am because you never listen!" In any case, don't stay on the phone with her to try and determine if she is or she isn't really suicidal; not only will this reward her manipulative behavior, you are not qualified to make that call. Even if you are a behavioral health professional, you are way too close to the situation to accurately assess anything, and you need a skilled third party—a.k.a.: the crisis line operator, to determine if her life really is in jeopardy.

The other obvious benefit is that your actions could save her life! In the chance that she is seriously thinking about suicide, the crisis team (**NOT you**) can get her the proper help. Because if she does attempt suicide, you can know in your heart that you did the right thing by calling in the professionals.

Note, too, that some very manipulative girls do "bogus" suicide attempts for attention—such as superficial cuts on their wrist or taking more than prescribed doses of medications—but flushing the majority of it first to make it look like they took much more than they actually did. Remember—*you do not need to be the one to determine if she is serious or just manipulating you with her suicide threats.* Simply make the phone call and leave it to the professionals. YOU'RE DONE HERE.

Do not hesitate to call the crisis line. Generally, these are publicly funded, and the operators are highly trained at gathering information and making a determination as to whether or not the threat is viable.

Further, if your ex does make an attempt on her life (bogus or actual), and you haven't done anything to try to get her help or told anyone in her family of her possibly being dangerous to herself, then guess who gets dubbed a "pig" and a "jerk" and a "no-good-lousy-ex-boyfriend who ruined my daughter's life!?" Yep. The nice guy who was just trying to lie low, keep her from freaking out, and weather the storm. You don't need to do that anymore. You just need to behave in a way that is both supportive and integral.

Last but not least, this approach shows Darla and her family/ friends that you really do care about her—enough to take steps necessary to keep her safe. At the same time, it demonstrates that you aren't going to be manipulated by such threats.

Okay... so are we clear on what to do if she pulls the suicide card? Good. What's next? Oh yeah...... that... (Don't worry... I've still got your hand...)

Jungle Beast #4: "You gave me an STD!

This is a really common accusation after a breakup. It seems so far fetched and completely ridiculous—yet many men have reported to me that they have had at least one ex girlfriend pull the "You game me an sexually transmitted disease!" card after a breakup.

To understand her momentary insanity, we need to look underneath the accusation. What is her goal of making such an accusation? What is her hidden agenda? We barely scratch the surface, and discover our answer.

She does this, first of all, because she just wants your attention, and this accusation is sure to get it. Secondly, she says this to keep you from sleeping with other women. The solution is simple: make an appointment with your doctor and get tested. The tests will likely come back negative. Send her a text or an email: *Got test results. No STD. Please leave me alone.*

Please… do NOT write, *You must have got it from your other boyfriend, you ho bag.* Or, *You psycho bitch, I didn't give you no STD. What the fuck is your problem?*

Don't post anything on her social media page or tell her friends that she accused you of giving her an STD. Again, just simply write, *Got test results back. No STD. Please leave me alone.*

Don't waste your time or energy trying to talk sense into her. Because she isn't in the sensible part of her mind, and you will just encourage her to keep contacting you.

Jungle Beast #5: " I'm Pregnant!"

The other thing that broken-hearted needy girls do is pull the *Oh my God! I'm pregnant!* card shortly after you break up with her. And you, being the nice, trusting guy you are, never question whether or not she is telling the truth. After your initial shock wears off, you decide to do the "right thing" and "try to make the relationship work... for the baby's sake." If she really isn't pregnant, which is often the case, she will have sex with you and try to get pregnant. (If you do have sex with her, use condoms until you know for sure whether she is or not). After sex, make sure you throw out the condom yourself... and then take the trash out to the curb. I've twice heard of a woman plucking up the freshly used condom off of the bed and shoving it into her vagina after her boyfriend left the bedroom.) YES! It happens. A desperate woman will do anything to secure a relationship. You need to watch out for them!) True, most condoms have spermicidal lube on them, but, of course, this is not 100% effective. If she doesn't get pregnant within a few months? You're still not off the hook: she fakes a miscarriage and you are roped into the task of comforting her through that crisis, and then trying to dump her afterwards, at which point she will squawk, "I can't believe he dumped me after my miscarriage! What a fucking bastard! And you've got the whole "pig" thing starting again. Still— break up with her as soon as possible after her (real or alleged) miscarriage—especially if you haven't magically fallen in love with her over the course of your recent time together.

Other Tricks a Woman May Use to Get Pregnant:

- While the condoms are still in the package, she uses a needle to poke holes in them

- She will tell men she is on birth control when she really isn't

- She uses an ovulation predictor (unbeknownst to him) and time sex with him to optimize the probability of pregnancy

Yes, I know... these kinds of situations are shocking, appalling, and sad, but they do happen. A heartbroken female will sometimes go to extreme measures and do whatever she can to stay with the man she loves—even if he doesn't love her back.

Here's what you do if your ex girlfriend suddenly pulls the "Oh my God! I'm pregnant!" card. First and foremost, find out if she really is pregnant! Ask her to make a doctor's appointment and tell her you want to go with her to that appointment. Then go with her. If she says she already went to the OBGYN and you're not allowed to go with her (for any reason) be very suspicious. Ask her (calmly—not accusingly) if you could please have her doctor's name and number so you can discuss the pregnancy with the doctor. (Beware that she will need to sign a Release of Information at the doctor's office in order for you to talk to any medical staff). If she says, "Why do you want to talk to the doctor? Don't you believe me? What the hell! As IF I would lie about something like this!"

Just stay calm. Simply reply, "I'm not saying I don't believe you. But if I am a father, I have the right to talk to the doctor about my unborn child." That is all you need to say. Insist on talking to the doctor, and don't let it go.

If you find out that she is really pregnant, then you obviously have other life decisions to make. But know that unplanned pregnancy is a really bad reason to marry someone. The proverbial "shotgun wedding" can make a man very resentful and make a messy mess even messier. However, in that situation, you are potentially a father now, and it's important to step into that and do what is best for your unborn child. That doesn't mean you should marry a woman you aren't in love with (for that's the "living a lie" thing again...) And I am not recommending that you two move in together. In fact, there are many reasons why you should not. But until paternity can be determined, I am recommending that you do your best to support her.

I know... the situation seems really unfair. Keep stress to a minimum—for all three of you: you, her, and the unborn baby. Do what you can to help her pay for medical care, nutritious food, and baby stuff. I strongly recommend against pressurizing her to get an abortion. Not only could that lead to emotional struggles later for you, it could lead to tremendous resentment from her. Remind yourself that this is a human life who deserves a fair chance.

Another piece of advice to the good guy: get a paternity test to make 100% certain that the child is yours. There is new DNA-testing technology available that can determine paternity of an unborn baby after a woman is in her tenth week of pregnancy. The tests can be pretty pricy, but are definitely worth it. Do an internet search on "paternity test while still pregnant" to find more information.

But if you can't afford pre-birth paternity testing, or she is not willing to submit to pre-birth paternity testing, you may need to wait until after the baby is born. You don't need to make it blatantly obvious to the whole fam damily, but just to the doctors and/or nurses assisting with the delivery, or, if you miss that opportunity, the pediatrician at the first wellness check. You can also buy home paternity kits at the local drug store, over the counter, next to the family planning section. Try to be discrete about it when testing, and try not to "wig out" when you get the results—whatever they are.

Again, the good guy will think, "Oh—she would never..." And truthfully, most girls wouldn't. But for every one hundred integral women, there are a handful of unscrupulous and scheming ones... who often make their way into the good guy's life. And often, until situations unfold that show her true colors, a man just can't tell which woman is integral and which one isn't.

In fact, exactly one week ago today (at the time of this writing) I talked to a 17 year old young man who found out that the baby his girlfriend told him was his—who just turned a year old—was, in fact, not his. And she knew the baby wasn't his from the time she got pregnant. But she was "madly in love with him, so chose him instead of the real father." This young man is understandably devastated—as he had formed a strong emotional bond with this child. At the same time, he despised this young lady for invading his life. And we can guess for certain that the child is equally, if not more devastated to have his "daddy" suddenly gone from his life—through no fault of his. Heart-breaking. On the other hand, this 17 year old young man is greatly relieved. This girl had made his life a living hell, nearly from the moment she stepped onto the scene. She has instigated a ton of chaos which could have been at least partially avoided if he would have gone with his gut instinct and ordered a paternity test before (if he could afford it) or soon after the baby was born. Instead, he made the decision to put 100% faith into his ex girlfriends word (that's what a good guy does... right?) that the baby really was his... I mean, no one would ever lie about something so huge. Well...???

It is also a possibility that, instead of stepping up as this 17 year old kid did in the example above, you may be tempted to resist, ignore, hide from your pregnant ex and claim, "it isn't mine!" when you don't, in fact, know for sure if it is or not. This behavior can easily label you a "pig" and create even more devastating consequences for you. Because, what will happen, is she will force you to take a paternity test through the courts, and the results will be virtually "broadcast" to all involved. It is much better not to hide during the pregnancy, and then be put through that humiliating process.

Because that will be used against you later in court if it is discovered that you are, indeed, the father and she fights for custody. So if there is a chance that the baby is yours, and as much as it bites, step up for the nine months it takes. Discretely get a paternity test—before if possible, or after the baby is born. It's just a much more grown-up way to go about things. Then, if the child is yours, you won't feel guilty for the rest of your life that you weren't there for him during his mama's pregnancy. And if he isn't yours, then you can walk away knowing that you did the grown-up thing and supported a woman who may have been carrying your child. No pig label here!

One more thing—if you find out that the woman lied to you, and the baby is not yours, do not verbally abash her, call her a whore, lying slut, whatever. Yes, it is absolutely infuriating, but she will have plenty of other problems to contend with in her life, and is now dealing with losing you in the process too. So you taking out your anger on her will not only further her emotional problems, it will directly affect her innocent infant. Be the big boy. And walk away as calmly as possible. No cussing. No slandering. Just maturity. And wishing her and the baby well as you part. Then pat yourself on the back for a job well done, and go out with friends to celebrate.

Besides those feelings of anger and resentment towards her for putting you through such an ordeal, don't be surprised if you feel sadness or grief if you find out the baby isn't yours. Those feelings are normal.

I wish I could tell you that grief, anger, and resentment are not a part of life. But they most certainly are. In any case, keep this in mind: you are now much wiser, and will choose your girlfriends much more carefully from now on. Which brings me to our next section:

Jungle Beast #7: The "Psycho Chick!"

(Don't worry, I've still got your hand!) The phrase "Psycho Chick" is kind of a catch-all—and to be honest, I don't really like the term, because it is very degrading. However, I am using it in this book because it is easily recognized and identified by men, and, my goal here is to keep you safe and thriving.

In the beginning of a relationship, a "psycho chick" isn't that easy to spot. It isn't until the relationship progresses that she starts to shows her true colors. Otherwise, of course, men would never get tangled up with women like this in the first place.

When someone refers to a "psycho chick," he or she is usually referring to someone who has what is known as a personality disorder. Personality disorders are clinically very difficult to treat, and the chaos and destruction usually show up within intimate relationships. Very briefly, the main personality disorders are:

Borderline Personality Disorder (BPD): Notated by an adult acting like a two year old: throwing tantrums. Also notated by extreme manipulation, ultra emotional sensitivity, excessive blame, and irrationality. BPD is very difficult to treat clinically. Due to the excessive mood swings, BPD is often confused with Bi-Polar Disorder, which is not a personality disorder, but a Mood Disorder, and therefore, clinically treatable.

Narcissistic Personality Disorder (NPD): Notated by people who think they are superior to others. Extreme conceit.

Dissociative Identity Disorder (DID): This used to be called Multiple Personality Disorder, whereby an adult person has two or more distinct personalities who are unaware the other personalities exist within them.

Antisocial Personality Disorder (APD): Destructive, hurtful, and just plain mean. Think "serial killer." This is more common in males, but women can be afflicted. People with APD can come across as charismatic and charming, making them extremely dangerous.

I also want to warn my readers, however, about the perils of becoming entangled with a sociopath. A sociopath is someone who has the inability to feel guilt or remorse for hurtful actions. Most sociopaths secretly have an unrelenting desire to cause chaos and destruction in other people's lives.

A psychopath is not an official DSM-IV term. I always think of a psychopath as a watered-down version of the sociopath—someone with no sense of remorse, who uses others for personal gain. Psychopaths can also come across as extremely charismatic, charming, and kind. They do this to gain the trust of others before exploiting them.

One out of every 25 people on the planet are sociopaths. One out of every 25. That means that, if you work in an organization of 300 people, then 12 of them are sociopaths. It also means that you could very likely end up dating one.

Sociopaths are masters of manipulation. Again, the scariest part is that they usually come across as caring, kind, loving, and friendly. But they use these traits for the deeper hunger of bringing chaos and destruction to other people's lives. Sociopaths have the potential to cause colossal destruction and chaos within the context of romantic relationships—especially for the good guy.

My sweet friend Ryan experienced this first hand. Ryan is extremely intelligent and very, successful—so don't think that "only stupid people" fall for sociopaths. Ryan met Stacy at a party three months ago; she was sweet, fun-loving, and "drop dead gorgeous." They started dating and, on the second date, as Ryan explained, they had "off the charts sex, like nothing I even thought was possible. I fell for her hard. And wanted more."

But after about a week, Stacy started asking about moving in together. As Ryan explained, "It kinda spooked me. But I still didn't think anything was wrong with her." Ryan was hesitant at first but their chemistry was "totally insane" and Stacy was "so darn sweet and sincere that I just couldn't say no to her." So just shy of two weeks after meeting, Stacy moved in with him.

Fast forward two months and we find Ryan's life in utter chaos. One week after moving in, Stacy quit her job and spent her days lounging by the pool and shopping... using his credit cards. Ryan spent thousands of dollars paying off her personal debt that she had before ever meeting him... and now she was racking up even more debt? WTF?? And when Ryan called her out on it, she completely flipped her lid and started crying and yelling at him.

"She also started getting really upset with the tiniest little things and manipulating my words... and even my thoughts. Like, once I called her "Baby" when we were having sex and she started crying, asking me who I was thinking about. It like, didn't even make sense. She made me feel like absolute shit about myself, and I didn't do anything wrong!" Ryan knew something was "really screwy" when he started dreading his rides home from work; he never knew what she was going to hit him with when he walked in the door. He always felt like he was "walking on eggshells" in his own house, and was on an insatiable quest to please her. He bought her a new laptop, took her out to nice dinners almost nightly, and she had somehow finagled him to let her continue to shop with his credit cards "as long as she didn't go over a certain amount." In short, Ryan gave Stacy "anything and everything she wanted, and it just wasn't enough to keep her happy. "She always found something I wasn't doing right, and seriously made me question my sanity."

Believe it or not, that isn't the worst part about Ryan's rendezvous with Stacy. After she was integrated into his group of friends, he started noticing something odd; several of his life-long buddies quit hanging out with him, for seemingly no reason. Some de-friended him from all social media, and one of his really good friends, as he put it, "totally unleashed on me, wanted to fight me and kept raging at me—saying, 'I know what you did! You fucking bastard!' I had NO idea what he was even talking about. I thought he was having like, a mental breakdown or something!"

During that rant, his friend accused him of sleeping with his girl-friend, Gina—which Ryan never did... but his friend refused to listen to him. "Don't even fucking lie! I told Stacy I wouldn't say anything to you, but how can I not?"

Ryan was stunned. "Stacy told you that I slept with Gina?"

When Ryan confronted Stacy about it, she denied everything, saying that Brian was "totally hitting on her one night, and he was really pissed that she told him to keep his hands to himself, so he was probably just making shit up to get back at her." Ryan knew that Brian would never try to hit on Stacy... any more than he would ever sleep with Gina. This is when he started realizing that Stacy was "really messed up in the head."

Slowly, after trying to make sense of these bizarre and twisting tales, the truth began to out; Stacy had been "innocently" telling horrible lies about Ryan to all of his friends, and she passed these lies off in casual conversation. For example, she told Ryan's friend Mark that "Ryan feels soooo bad for making out with Jane two years ago... right before your wedding. Oops! Sorry! I thought you knew?! Well don't tell him I said anything. He feels really bad about it." You can imagine the kind of destruction Stacy was able to cause in just two months of being in his life; her "destruction operatives" were so covert, and all of his friends were so taken with her charm and kind nature, they never thought for a second that she was capable of anything but genuineness and integrity.

Note that Ryan felt "really bad for Stacy because something was obviously really wrong with her." In fact, this is the reason he never fully broke off the relationship after the truth started emerging. Ryan tried to break up with her several times, but she simply wouldn't leave his house. When he threatened to call the cops, Stacy would turn on the water-works and sob convincingly about being "so sorry for everything!" And would he "please give her another chance?" Which Ryan did, many times. But things never improved. Every time he would make his resolve to boot her out anyway, she would sob hysterically that she had nowhere else to go; her family abandoned her and she had no friends. She sobbed about her rough childhood, about her mother abandoning her, and that she was so grateful to him for teaching her how to love. She would tell him, "I just love you so much! Thank you for being here for me and believing in me when no body else would!"

As Ryan explains it, "She was so damn convincing!" YES, sociopaths usually are. Ryan gave Stacy chance after chance, with the hopes that he would be able to help her come to terms with her awful past and live a better life. Of course, every tear she cried, every sob into his supporting shoulder, and every word she spoke were all contrived... meant solely for the means of appropriating his money, peace of mind, and energy. This, my good readers, is a perfect depiction of a sociopath. And with one in 25 people being a sociopath, chances are that you are dealing with at least one (if not more) in your life right now, on one level or another. And chances are even better that you have (or will) run across one or two in your romantic life. Beware.

Ryan finally was able to successfully break up with her, but not before she nearly destroyed his life. He will never know the extent of the lies Stacy told about him; many of his friends won't return his calls and his explanations about Stacy being "the crazy type of person she is" has fallen on angry ears. Stacy blamed Ryan for her debt, had extremely poor emotional control, and imposed massive amounts of guilt on him for "the stupidest things." Ryan is worried about other guys that might date her, "But there's nothing I can do about it."

Until a recent conversation with me about sociopaths and personality disorders, Ryan had no words for what even happened with her. He was actually relieved after we talked. "It doesn't undo what she's done to my life. But at least now I have an explanation for it, and I can stop blaming myself."

Sociopaths tend to gravitate towards kindhearted and giving people (they are easier to exploit than others). So if you are the type of person who has a hard time "abandoning" a person in need—whose life seems to be one chaotic disaster after another—to the point that it has taken a substantial amount of time, money, and peace of mind from you, I encourage you to adapt a new thought: *I will pray for her, but get away from her.* You can't fix a girl like this. Don't waste your life trying. Just get out. And get as far away from her as possible.

60 Signs of a "Psycho Chick"

Again, I don't like the term "psycho chick" because it is a cliché label that is way overused; often, women who are trying to ditch needy men get categorized as *psycho,* and the term, itself, is pretty degrading. Still, my goal here is to educate you on keeping yourself safe from girls who could cause true damage in your life—and on many levels. This list is not a diagnostic tool, and this list is not exhaustive. Further, just because a girl embodies a few of these traits, it does not make her "psycho." Please read this list with that in mind:

1. The proverbial "psycho chick" is often extremely beautiful or charming

2. She uses her beauty and charm to get her way

3. She shows up at your place, unannounced

4. She has crazy, off-the-charts sex with you

5. She acts like you owe her an explanation for things that are none of her business

6. She parties a lot and lives a hedonistic (pleasure-seeking) lifestyle

7. She pushes you for a commitment, an engagement ring, or marriage

8. She has no personal life goals

9. She has previous arrests for violence

10. She has previous restraining orders against her

11. She shows up at your favorite hangouts and pretends it's a coincidence

12. She goes through your phone and / or wallet when you are sleeping or showering

13. She tries to hack into your email or social media page

14. She says, "I don't know what I would ever do if we broke up!" far too often.

15. She wants to move in with you right away (sooner than six months)

16. She wants to meet your family right away

17. She shows signs of low self-esteem

18. She seems shallow and materialistic

19. She "punishes" you with emotional tantrums or mood swings

20. She has tantrums in public

21. She expects you to pay for everything

22. She wants you to take care of her financially

23. She lies or exaggerates the truth

24. She looks for signs that you've been with other women on your clothes, in your car, in your house, etc...

25. She has a "mean streak" that she passes off as a sign of "independence"

26. She has moments of extreme kindness and moments of extreme rudeness / meanness

27. She is sarcastic or insulting, then plays it off as "a joke"

28. She accuses you of being "too sensitive" when she hurts your feelings

29. She physically hits you (hard) and then passes it off as "just being playful" or "just goofing around"

30. She delivers the "cold shoulder" and is silently controlling

31. She has significant mood swings (laughing one minute / crying the next)

32. She causes problems between you and your friends

33. She flirts with your friends

34. She hates your friends

35. She sleeps with your friends (or tries to)

36. She makes you feel guilty over nothing

37. She hates her parents

38. She flirts with other men in your presence

39. She always play the victim

40. She drinks excessively or uses drugs

41. She is on several different psychiatric medications and takes them inconsistently

42. She acts like life is horribly unfair

43. She blames her family, ex boyfriend, ex boss, etc... for her problems

44. She blames you for her problems

45. She complains and gripes about people—including you

46. She shows signs of being delusional (making up conversations that you never had, accusing you of doing things you've never done, or she can't explain how things happened—like where the money in your wallet went, how the car fender got dented, or how a mirror in the hall got broken)

47. She shows signs of extreme jealousy

48. She doesn't give straight answers to straightforward questions

49. She sends mixed messages and expects you to "read her mind" then gets mad when you fail to do so

50. She wants a lavish lifestyle but has little money of her own

51. She acts insecure around other beautiful women (e.g.: she accuses you of looking at other women)

52. She is manipulative

53. She twists your words and throws them back in your face

54. She makes you feel very confused during conversations

55. She is emotionally needy and you are scared to "trigger" her

56. She makes physical threats against you—sometimes in jest

57. She makes physical threats against herself

58. She calls and texts you far too much

59. She discourages you from hanging out with your friends, especially other girls

60. She keeps you on an emotional "leash"—and you have very little freedom in your life since meeting her

Again, this list is not a diagnostic tool, but a quick checklist ONLY.

To break up with a sociopath (or someone you suspect is a sociopath) follow the rules for breakups discussed above. You're just going to have to be much more tenacious about it. Don't hesitate to call the police if she destroys property or threatens to hurt you.

As a side note, I do NOT recommend going to couple's counseling with a sociopath—or even a girl you suspect might be a sociopath—because (and this is coming from a former counselor) such girls are usually very skilled at coming across as the victim and making you look like a horrible person. A counselor only sees you once a week or so. A counselor doesn't live day in and day out with you, and only sees what goes on in session. Further, if she is unskilled, uneducated about personality disorders (many are), inexperienced, or bitter toward men herself, she will side with your psycho girl, and you will just end up wasting your time and money, and peace of mind.

Aaaannnd... CLEAR!

Okay, Sir—that's it for the Jungle Beasts! WHEW! We are out of the woods!

<Shake it off... shake it off...>

And... can I have my hand back? ☺

Okay... Back to the Fun Stuff

Yes, just about ANY man can get just about ANY woman to fall for him. This means that you can get HER (yes... HER) to fall for you. This is not some sappy, far-off, or smoke-blowing claim... I make this statement confidently. It all comes down to abiding by the simple physics of attraction. This "physics of attraction" embodies your attitudes, your energy, your belief systems, and behaviors that form your presence in the world... and how you show up with women. In the right combination, everything works.

Professor Williams

For those of you who still think romance, getting lucky, and love are all about looks, sculpted muscles, and having a bunch of money, here's your reality check. I've seen incredibly beautiful, intelligent women fall hard for the most unlikely of men.

Years ago, I had a professor in college—one of my favorite professors of all time, in fact—Professor Williams. Professor Williams was born with a genetic skeletal condition called Cleidocranial Dysostosis, which causes cranial (head) and skeletal (bone) deformities. He had considerable physical limitations (e.g.: he was born without collarbones, he couldn't bend his elbows or knees, and his legs were deformed). He was able to walk with the help of arm braces, was quite independent, and very, very intelligent.

Professor Williams had every reason in the world to believe that the cards were stacked against him in the world of romance... but he never fell for that belief. Lo—Professor Williams had a beautiful, devoted wife who was so crazy in love with him that she couldn't see straight. Deformities and all. Physical limitations and all. She adored him. He often brought pictures of his family to show our class and was obviously in love with her too.

Professor Williams didn't have the looks of a G.Q. model. Far from it. He didn't have the physique of a professional body builder. He needed to pull his socks up with "grabbers on sticks" for God's sake. While he was well-established in his career, he didn't have a bank account that afforded him a life of luxury. What on God's green earth did his wife see in him??

Quite simply, Professor Williams had an incredible presence about him. In spite of his physical condition—or, as he would tell you—

because of it, he was extremely grateful for everything in his life. This was evident in his demeanor as he constantly radiated joy. When we are happy within ourselves, it means that we love ourselves. When we love ourselves, everyone else loves us too.

In fact, everything about Professor Williams radiated joy and confidence. He would even poke fun at himself and often had our whole class rolling on the floor laughing with his hilarious life stories. Sometimes he would get completely distracted from the curriculum, and would go off on story tangents for an hour or more. And we loved it, and no one dared interrupted him! Here's an example: one evening, our lecture was about peer pressure, and the psychological importance of feeling safe and respected in the social setting. He segued into the story about his own youth, and the day in junior high that he finally stood up to the bullies that had brutally tortured him on an almost daily basis since kindergarten. Because he couldn't bend his elbows and had hyper contraction in his muscles, he figured out that he could "hit 'em really hard under the chin and knock their damn blocks off!" From that day forward, whenever a bully threatened him, he would "wobble toward him as fast as he could, start shrieking like a mad man and swing his 'built in nightstick' up and down until it landed under their chin. WHAMMO! The bullies were suddenly terrified of him—and with good reason; he spent the rest of his junior high school days "randomly whacking all the kids who had ever bullied him under the chin when they passed him in the hall." Sometimes he would knock them so hard they would lose a few teeth. He dislocated more than one jaw. He knocked most of the (former) bullies clean onto their asses. "Of course, no one ever ratted me out to the teachers. I mean, who wants to admit that they were just beat up by the gimpy kid who can't bend his elbows?! But believe you-me that all the kids in the school knew it! But the nurse couldn't figure out what the hell was goin' on. I mean, every other day another kid would land in her office with a dislocated jaw or missing teeth!" We ROARED— laughing so hard we were crying and had stomach pains. He explained, "Standing up to those bullies was necessary for my confidence level. But by the time I got to high school, my chin-whacking days were behind me, and most of the bullies became my friends."

It doesn't end there. In college, girls started paying attention to him. Not only was he extremely smart and made excellent grades, he was "so goofy and carefree about life that everyone wanted to just hang out! Everyone else was just so uptight about everything, worried about grades, sports, and whatever. Me? I was just happy to be alive. I mean, the doctors didn't even think I'd live past a year, so I figure every day has been a gift!" He went on to explain, "For some reason, dating was easy for me. I never could figure out what the girls saw in me. I mean, look at me! I'm a gnarly mess! But boy, howdy, they would come over to 'study' with me, and I had the time of my life! And usually those girls were dating these big, muscle-y jock boyfriends. But the guys never suspected a thing because they would take one look at me and assume I never had been with a girl in my life, and that their gorgeous gal wouldn't be interested in a twisted up runt like me. Little did they know that we'd burn up the sheets and then some. And I'll tell you, the dorm maintenance guy was getting tired my bed popping springs and loosing nuts and bolts, ya know what I mean?" (HA! HA!! OUCH! MY STOMACH!)

Professor Williams met his wife in his Master's program, and that's when he "stopped hobbling around and chasing skirts" (ROLF!) because he knew he had found *the one*. His wife came to our class one day when we had a quasi-famous guest speaker whom she wanted to see present. It was obvious to all how much she loved Professor Williams! She could barely take her eyes off him.

Indeed, Professor Williams had somehow figured out the mystery behind physical and attraction and romance: confidence, attitude, energy, and joy. Guess what? So can you. I learned so much about life from him about the importance of embracing your perceived flaws and making them work for you. He was an excellent professor and a huge inspiration.

Learn from his story. Don't sell yourself short. Embrace everything about yourself. Sexual chemistry is never a matter of looks, muscles, or money; it is a matter of attitude, emotional "leverage" and know-how that a man brings into the wild and crazy world of women. Men who are successful when it comes to romance, like Professor Williams, hold to specific principles of love and attraction—

sometimes unknowingly—and men who are unsuccessful in romance, very simply, don't.

Dude. I Promise. You've Got This

And now, my good man, you've got all the secrets! You've got everything it takes to attract, engage, date, and love the woman of your dreams. Now do me proud and go get her!

About the Author: Aaliyah Dahlia

Aaliyah Dahlia has a Master's degree in Family Counseling and eight years experience as a couple's counselor. She has worked with women and men alike. Aaliyah dedicates Tapping into Chicks to her late baby brother, Johnny—the true girl-wooing guru behind this book. Since stepping onto the dating scene in his mid-teens, Johnny was the ultimate girl-magnet. Why? With four older sisters and three foster sisters—all just a few years older than him—he was raised in "estrogen boot camp." This gave him the unique opportunity to observe seven plutonic females in his immediate living environment navigate their way through their own romantic adventures. By deciphering the subtle "female seduction code" that imparted John his romantic-savvy, Aaliyah gives men a simple, effective plan for dating success. Her easy-to-follow advice will inspire even the most timid of men into confident female interaction. Tapping into Chicks series is a must-read for any man looking to boost his success factor with women!

Dedicated To Johnny

It is with utmost respect and admiration that I dedicate this book to my baby brother Johnny. Rest in eternal peace, brother. We love you and miss you every day!

www.ingramcontent.com/pod-product-compliance
Lightning Source LLC
Chambersburg PA
CBHW071541040426
42452CB00008B/1082